CRIMINAL PROCEDURE

2022 Case and Statutory Supplement

CRIMINAL PROCEDURE

2022 Case and Statutory Supplement

Erwin Chemerinsky

Dean and Jesse H. Choper Distinguished Professor of Law
University of California, Berkeley School of Law

Laurie L. Levenson

Professor of Law and
David W. Burcham Chair in Ethical Advocacy
Loyola Law School

ASPEN PUBLISHING

To contact Customer Service, e-mail customer.service@aspenpublishing.com, call 1-800-950-5259, or mail correspondence to:

Aspen Publishing
Attn: Order Department
PO Box 990
Frederick, MD 21705

Printed in the United States of America.

1 2 3 4 5 6 7 8 9 0

ISBN 978-1-5438-5883-9

About Aspen Publishing

Aspen Publishing is a leading provider of educational content and digital learning solutions to law schools in the U.S. and around the world. Aspen provides best-in-class solutions for legal education through authoritative textbooks, written by renowned authors, and breakthrough products such as Connected eBooks, Connected Quizzing, and PracticePerfect.

The Aspen Casebook Series (famously known among law faculty and students as the "red and black" casebooks) encompasses hundreds of highly regarded textbooks in more than eighty disciplines, from large enrollment courses, such as Torts and Contracts to emerging electives such as Sustainability and the Law of Policing. Study aids such as the *Examples & Explanations* and the *Emanuel Law Outlines* series, both highly popular collections, help law students master complex subject matter.

Major products, programs, and initiatives include:

- **Connected eBooks** are enhanced digital textbooks and study aids that come with a suite of online content and learning tools designed to maximize student success. Designed in collaboration with hundreds of faculty and students, the Connected eBook is a significant leap forward in the legal education learning tools available to students.

- **Connected Quizzing** is an easy-to-use formative assessment tool that tests law students' understanding and provides timely feedback to improve learning outcomes. Delivered through CasebookConnect.com, the learning platform already used by students to access their Aspen casebooks, Connected Quizzing is simple to implement and integrates seamlessly with law school course curricula.

- **PracticePerfect** is a visually engaging, interactive study aid to explain commonly encountered legal doctrines through easy-to-understand animated videos, illustrative examples, and numerous practice questions. Developed by a team of experts, PracticePerfect is the ideal study companion for today's law students.

- The **Aspen Learning Library** enables law schools to provide their students with access to the most popular study aids on the market across all of their courses. Available through an annual subscription, the online library consists of study aids in e-book, audio, and video formats with full text search, note-taking, and highlighting capabilities.

- Aspen's **Digital Bookshelf** is an institutional-level online education bookshelf, consolidating everything students and professors need to ensure success. This program ensures that every student has access to affordable course materials from day one.

- **Leading Edge** is a community centered on thinking differently about legal education and putting those thoughts into actionable strategies. At the core of the program is the Leading Edge Conference, an annual gathering of legal education thought leaders looking to pool ideas and identify promising directions of exploration.

CONTENTS

Preface   *xi*

**Chapter 4. Police Interrogation and the Privilege Against
Self-Incrimination**   1
    B. Fifth Amendment Limits on Custodial Interrogation:
        Miranda v. Arizona   1
        1. Miranda v. Arizona and Its Affirmation by the
            Supreme Court   1
            Vega v. Tekoh   *1*

Chapter 9. Plea Bargaining and Guilty Pleas   11
    G. Impact of Guilty Pleas   11
        Class v. United States   *11*

Chapter 11. Right to Counsel   15
    D. Standard for "Effective Assistance" of Counsel   15
        Andrus v. Texas   *15*

Chapter 12. Trial by Jury   23
    B. Jury Composition and Selection   23
        2. Selecting the Petit Jury   23
            Flowers v. Mississippi   *23*
    C. Pretrial Publicity and the Right to a Fair Trial   30
        1. When Does Pretrial Publicity Interfere with a
            Defendant's Right to a Fair Trial?   30
            United States v. Tsarnaev   *30*

Chapter 13. Sentencing   35
    D. The Death Penalty   35
        3. Recent Limits on the Scope of the Death Penalty   35
            d. Method of Execution   35
                Bucklew v. Precythe   *35*

Chapter 14. Double Jeopardy   43
    D. Exceptions to the Double Jeopardy Rule   43
        2. Dual Sovereignty   43
            Denezpi v. United States   *43*

Chapter 15. Habeas Corpus   55

    B. The Issues that Must Be Addressed in Order for a
Federal Court to Grant Habeas Corpus Relief   55

       4. Does the Petition Rely on Existing Rules or Seek
Recognition of a New Rule of Constitutional Law?   55

          Edwards v. Vannoy   55

Federal Rules of Criminal Procedure   61

Rule 4.   Arrest Warrant or Summons on a Complaint   61

Rule 4.1.   Complaint, Warrant, or Summons by Telephone or Other
Reliable Electronic Means   63

Rule 5.   Initial Appearance   65

Rule 5.1.   Preliminary Hearing   68

Rule 6.   The Grand Jury   70

Rule 7.   The Indictment and the Information   76

Rule 8.   Joinder of Offenses or Defendants   77

Rule 11.   Pleas   78

Rule 14.   Relief from Prejudicial Joinder   82

Rule 16.   Discovery and Inspection   83

Rule 23.   Jury or Nonjury Trial   88

Rule 26.2.   Producing a Witness's Statement   89

Rule 41.   Search and Seizure   90

Excerpted Statutes   96

18 U.S.C.   96

§3142.   Release or Detention of a Defendant Pending Trial   96

§3144.   Release or Detention of a Material Witness   102

§3161.   Time Limits and Exclusions   102

28 U.S.C.   107

§2241.   Power to Grant Writ   107

§2242.   Application   108

§2243.   Issuance of Writ; Return; Hearing; Decision   109

§2244.   Finality of Determination   109

§2245.   Certificate of Trial Judge Admissible in Evidence   111

§2246.   Evidence; Depositions; Affidavits   111

§2247.   Documentary Evidence   111

§2248.   Return or Answer; Conclusiveness   112

§2249.   Certified Copies of Indictment, Plea and Judgment; Duty of
Respondent   112

§2250.   Indigent Petitioner Entitled to Documents Without Cost   112

§2251.   Stay of State Court Proceedings   112

§2252.   Notice   112

Contents

§2253. Appeal   113
§2254. State Custody; Remedies in State Courts   113
§2255. Federal Custody; Remedies on Motion Attacking Sentence   115
§2261. Prisoners in State Custody Subject to Capital Sentence;
        Appointment of Counsel; Requirement of Rule of Court or
        Statute; Procedures for Appointment   116
§2262. Mandatory Stay of Execution; Duration; Limits on Stays of
        Execution; Successive Petitions   117
§2263. Filing of Habeas Corpus Application; Time Requirements;
        Tolling Rules   118
§2264. Scope of Federal Review; District Court Adjudications   118
§2265. Certification and Judicial Review   119
§2266. Limitation Periods for Determining Applications and Motions   119

PREFACE

The fourth edition of the casebook was published in 2022 and includes cases decided through the end of October Term 2020, which finished on July 2, 2021. This Supplement is needed for a few reasons. It covers cases decided since publication of the fourth edition. Also, it is a statutory supplement providing statutory material related to each of the chapters.

We plan to do a supplement each year. Each will include the cases decided since the latest edition of the casebook was published, as well as the most recent version of this statutory material. We welcome comments and suggestions from the professors and students using our book.

Erwin Chemerinsky
Laurie Levenson

July 2022

CRIMINAL PROCEDURE

2022 Case and Statutory Supplement

Chapter 4

POLICE INTERROGATION AND THE PRIVILEGE AGAINST SELF-INCRIMINATION

B. Fifth Amendment Limits on Custodial Interrogation: Miranda v. Arizona

1. Miranda v. Arizona and Its Affirmation by the Supreme Court (casebook p. 590)

The usual remedy for a violation of *Miranda* is exclusion of the statements that were gained without proper warnings. But could an individual who was interrogated without warnings bring a civil suit for money damages? In *Chavez v. Martinez* (2003) (casebook pp. 606-607), the Court held that civil suits are not possible if the statements are not introduced into evidence against the suspect. But what if the statements are introduced? That is the issue in *Vega v. Tekoh* and the Court, in a 6-3 decision, held that civil suits for money damages are not permissible for *Miranda* violations, even when the statements are admitted at trial against the defendant. Both the majority and the dissent focus on how *Miranda v. Arizona* should be understood.

Vega v. Tekoh

142 S. Ct. ___ (2022)

Justice ALITO delivered the opinion of the Court.

This case presents the question whether a plaintiff may sue a police officer under 42 U.S.C. §1983, based on the allegedly improper admission of an "un-*Mirandized*" statement in a criminal prosecution. The case arose out of the interrogation of respondent, Terence Tekoh, by petitioner, Los Angeles County Sheriff 's Deputy Carlos Vega. Deputy Vega questioned Tekoh at his place of employment and did not give him a *Miranda* warning. Tekoh was prosecuted, and his confession was admitted into evidence, but the jury returned a verdict of not guilty. Tekoh then sued Vega under §1983, and the United States Court of Appeals for the Ninth Circuit held that the use of Tekoh's un-*Mirandized* statement provided a valid basis for a §1983 claim against Vega. We now reject this extension of our *Miranda* case law.

1

4. Police Interrogation and the Privilege Against Self-Incrimination

I

In March 2014, Tekoh was working as a certified nursing assistant at a Los Angeles medical center. When a female patient accused him of sexually assaulting her, the hospital staff reported the accusation to the Los Angeles County Sheriff 's Department, and Deputy Vega responded. Vega questioned Tekoh at length in the hospital, and Tekoh eventually provided a written statement apologizing for inappropriately touching the patient's genitals. The parties dispute whether Vega used coercive investigatory techniques to extract the statement, but it is undisputed that he never informed Tekoh of his rights under *Miranda v. Arizona* (1966), which held that during a custodial interrogation police officers must inform a suspect that "he has the right to remain silent, that anything he says can be used against him in a court of law, that he has the right to the presence of an attorney, and that if he cannot afford an attorney one will be appointed for him prior to any questioning."

Tekoh was arrested and charged in California state court with unlawful sexual penetration. At Tekoh's first trial, the judge held that *Miranda* had not been violated because Tekoh was not in custody when he provided the statement, but the trial resulted in a mistrial. When Tekoh was retried, a second judge again denied his request to exclude the confession. This trial resulted in acquittal, and Tekoh then brought this action under 42 U.S.C. §1983 against Vega and several other defendants seeking damages for alleged violations of his constitutional rights, including his Fifth Amendment right against compelled self-incrimination.

When this §1983 case was first tried, the jury returned a verdict in favor of Vega, but the judge concluded that he had given an improper jury instruction and thus granted a new trial. Before the second trial, Tekoh asked the court to instruct the jury that it was required to find that Vega violated the Fifth Amendment right against compelled self-incrimination if it determined that he took a statement from Tekoh in violation of *Miranda* and that the statement was then improperly used against Tekoh at his criminal trial. The District Court declined, reasoning that *Miranda* established a prophylactic rule and that such a rule could not alone provide a ground for §1983 liability. Instead, the jury was asked to decide whether Tekoh's Fifth Amendment right had been violated. The court instructed the jury to determine, based on "the totality of all the surrounding circumstances," whether Tekoh's statement had been "improperly coerced or compelled," and the court explained that "[a] confession is improperly coerced or compelled . . . if a police officer uses physical or psychological force or threats not permitted by law to undermine a person's ability to exercise his or her free will." The jury found in Vega's favor, and Tekoh appealed.

A Ninth Circuit panel reversed, holding that the "use of an un-*Mirandized* statement against a defendant in a criminal proceeding violates the Fifth Amendment and may support a §1983 claim" against the officer who obtained the statement. The panel thus remanded the case for a new trial.

4. Police Interrogation and the Privilege Against Self-Incrimination

II

Section 1983 provides a cause of action against any person acting under color of state law who "subjects" a person or "causes [a person] to be subjected . . . to the deprivation of any rights, privileges, or immunities secured by the Constitution and laws." The question we must decide is whether a violation of the *Miranda* rules provides a basis for a claim under §1983. We hold that it does not.

A

If a *Miranda* violation were tantamount to a violation of the Fifth Amendment, our answer would of course be different. The Fifth Amendment, made applicable to the States by the Fourteenth Amendment, provides that "[n]o person . . . shall be compelled in any criminal case to be a witness against himself." This Clause "permits a person to refuse to testify against himself at a criminal trial in which he is a defendant" and "also 'privileges him not to answer official questions put to him in any other proceeding, civil or criminal, formal or informal, where the answers might incriminate him in future criminal proceedings.'" In addition, the right bars the introduction against a criminal defendant of out-of-court statements obtained by compulsion.

In *Miranda*, the Court concluded that additional procedural protections were necessary to prevent the violation of this important right when suspects who are in custody are interrogated by the police. To afford this protection, the Court required that custodial interrogation be preceded by the now-familiar warnings mentioned above, and it directed that statements obtained in violation of these new rules may not be used by the prosecution in its case-in-chief.

In this case, the Ninth Circuit held—and Tekoh now argues, that a violation of *Miranda* constitutes a violation of the Fifth Amendment right against compelled self-incrimination, but that is wrong. *Miranda* itself and our subsequent cases make clear that *Miranda* imposed a set of prophylactic rules. Those rules, to be sure, are "constitutionally based," but they are prophylactic rules nonetheless.

B

Miranda itself was clear on this point. *Miranda* did not hold that a violation of the rules it established necessarily constitute a Fifth Amendment violation, and it is difficult to see how it could have held otherwise. For one thing, it is easy to imagine many situations in which an un-*Mirandized* suspect in custody may make self-incriminating statements without any hint of compulsion. In addition, the warnings that the Court required included components, such as notification of the right to have retained or appointed counsel present during questioning, that do not concern self-incrimination *per se* but are instead plainly designed to safeguard that right. And the same is true of *Miranda*'s detailed rules about the waiver of the right to remain silent and the right to an attorney.

At no point in the opinion did the Court state that a violation of its new rules constituted a violation of the Fifth Amendment right against compelled self-incrimination. Instead, it claimed only that those rules were needed to safe-guard that right during custodial interrogation. In accordance with this under-standing of the nature of the rules it imposed, the *Miranda* Court stated quite clearly that the Constitution did not itself require "adherence to any particular solution for the inherent compulsions of the interrogation process" and that its decision "in no way create[d] a constitutional straitjacket." The opinion added that its new rules might not be needed if Congress or the States adopted "other procedures which are at least as effective," *ibid.*, and the opinion suggested that there might not have been any actual Fifth Amendment violations in the four cases that were before the Court. The Court could not have said any of these things if a violation of the *Miranda* rules necessarily constituted a violation of the Fifth Amendment. Since *Miranda*, the Court has repeatedly described the rules it adopted as "prophylactic."

C

After *Miranda* was handed down, the Court engaged in the process of chart-ing the dimensions of these new prophylactic rules. As we would later spell out, this process entailed a weighing of the benefits and costs of any clarification of the rules' scope.

Some post-*Miranda* decisions found that the balance of interests justi-fied restrictions that would not have been possible if *Miranda* represented an explanation of the meaning of the Fifth Amendment right as opposed to a set of rules designed to protect that right. For example, in *Harris v. New York* (1971), the Court held that a statement obtained in violation of *Miranda* could be used to impeach the testimony of a defendant, even though an invol-untary statement obtained in violation of the Fifth Amendment could not have been employed in this way. Engaging in the process we described in *Shatzer*, the *Harris* Court considered the benefits of forbidding impeachment but dismissed "the speculative possibility" that this would discourage "imper-missible police conduct," and on the other side of the scale, it feared that barring impeachment would turn *Miranda* into "a license to use perjury by way of a defense."

A similar analysis was used in *Michigan v. Tucker* (1974), where the Court held that the "fruits" of an un-*Mirandized* statement can be admitted. The Court noted that "the 'fruits' of police conduct which actually infringe[s]" a defendant's constitutional rights must be suppressed. But the Court distinguished police con-duct that "abridge[s] [a person's] constitutional privilege against compulsory self-incrimination" from conduct that "depart[s] only from the prophylactic standards later laid down by this Court in *Miranda* to safeguard that privilege." Because there had been only a *Miranda* violation in that case, the *Wong Sun* rule of auto-matic exclusion was found to be inapplicable. Instead, the Court asked whether the *Miranda* rules' prophylactic purposes justified the exclusion of the fruits of the violation, and after "balancing the interests involved," it held that exclusion was not required.

4. Police Interrogation and the Privilege Against Self-Incrimination

In *New York v. Quarles* (1984), the Court held that statements obtained in violation of *Miranda* need not be suppressed when the questioning is conducted to address an ongoing "public safety" concern. The Court reasoned that *Miranda* warnings are "'not themselves rights protected by the Constitution'" and that "the need for answers to questions in a situation posing a threat to the public safety outweigh[ed] the need for the prophylactic rule."

Finally, in the Court again distinguished between a constitutional violation and a violation of *Miranda*. In that case, a suspect in custody was initially questioned without receiving a *Miranda* warning, and the statements made at that time were suppressed. But the suspect was later given *Miranda* warnings, chose to waive his *Miranda* rights, and signed a written confession. Asked to decide whether this confession was admissible, the Court followed the reasoning in *Tucker* and again held that the fruit-of-the-poisonous-tree rule that applies to constitutional violations does not apply to violations of *Miranda*. The Court refused to exclude the signed confession and emphasized that an officer's error "in administering the prophylactic *Miranda* procedures . . . should not breed the same irremediable consequences as police infringement of the Fifth Amendment itself."

It is hard to see how these decisions could stand if a violation of *Miranda* constituted a violation of the Fifth Amendment.

D

While these decisions imposed limits on *Miranda*'s prophylactic rules, other decisions found that the balance of interests called for expansion. In *Doyle v. Ohio* (1976), the Court held that silence following a *Miranda* warning cannot be used to impeach. The Court acknowledged that *Miranda* warnings are "prophylactic," and it recognized the prosecution's need to test a defendant's exculpatory story through cross-examination. But it found that allowing the use of post-warning silence would undermine the warnings' implicit promise that silence would not be used to convict.

Similarly, in *Roberson*, the Court held that a suspect's post-warning request for counsel with respect to one offense barred later interrogation without counsel regarding a different offense. Describing the *Miranda* rules as "prophylactic protections," the Court concluded that both law enforcement and criminal defendants would benefit from a bright-line.

Finally, in *Withrow v. Williams*, the Court rejected an attempt to restrict *Miranda*'s application in collateral proceedings based on the reasoning in *Stone v. Powell* (1976). In *Stone*, the Court had held that a defendant who has had a full and fair opportunity to seek suppression of evidence allegedly seized in violation of the Fourth Amendment may not obtain federal habeas relief on that ground, and in *Withrow*, a state prison warden argued that a similar rule should apply to a habeas petitioner who had been given an opportunity to litigate a *Miranda* claim at trial. Once again acknowledging that *Miranda* adopted prophylactic rules, the Court balanced the competing interests and found that the costs of adopting the warden's argument outweighed any benefits. On the cost side, the Court noted that enforcing *Miranda* "safeguards 'a fundamental *trial* right'" and furthers "the correct ascertainment of guilt" at trial. And on the other side, the Court found that the adoption of a *Stone*-like rule "would not significantly benefit the federal courts in their exercise of habeas jurisdiction, or advance the cause of federalism in any substantial way."

Thus, all the post-*Miranda* cases we have discussed acknowledged the prophylactic nature of the *Miranda* rules and engaged in cost-benefit analysis to define the scope of these prophylactic rules.

E

Contrary to the decision below and Tekoh's argument here, our decision in did not upset the firmly established prior understanding of *Miranda* as a prophylactic decision. *Dickerson* involved a federal statute, 18 U.S.C. §3501, that effectively overruled *Miranda* by making the admissibility of a statement given during custodial interrogation turn solely on whether it was made voluntarily. The Court held that Congress could not abrogate *Miranda* by statute because *Miranda* was a "constitutional decision" that adopted a "constitutional rule," and the Court noted that these rules could not have been made applicable to the States if it did not have that status.

At the same time, however, the Court made it clear that it was not equating a violation of the *Miranda* rules with an outright Fifth Amendment violation. For one thing, it reiterated *Miranda*'s observation that "the Constitution would not preclude legislative solutions that differed from the prescribed *Miranda* warnings but which were 'at least as effective in apprising accused persons'" of their rights.

Even more to the point, the Court rejected the dissent's argument that §3501 could not be held unconstitutional unless "*Miranda* warnings are required by the Constitution, in the sense that nothing else will suffice to satisfy constitutional requirements." The Court's answer, in substance, was that the *Miranda* rules, though not an explication of the meaning of the Fifth Amendment right, are rules that are necessary to protect that right (at least until a better alternative is found and adopted). Thus, in the words of the *Dickerson* Court, the *Miranda* rules are "constitutionally based" and have "constitutional underpinnings." But the obvious point of these formulations was to avoid saying that a *Miranda* violation is the same as a violation of the Fifth Amendment right.

What all this boils down to is basically as follows. The *Miranda* rules are prophylactic rules that the Court found to be necessary to protect the Fifth Amendment right against compelled self-incrimination. In that sense, *Miranda* was a "constitutional decision" and it adopted a "constitutional rule" because the decision was based on the Court's judgment about what is required to safeguard that constitutional right. And when the Court adopts a constitutional prophylactic rule of this nature, *Dickerson* concluded, the rule has the status of a "La[w] of the United States" that is binding on the States under the Supremacy Clause (as *Miranda* implicitly held, since three of the four decisions it reversed came from state court, and the rule cannot be altered by ordinary legislation.

4. Police Interrogation and the Privilege Against Self-Incrimination

This was a bold and controversial claim of authority, but we do not think that *Dickerson* can be understood any other way without (1) taking the insupportable position that a *Miranda* violation is tantamount to a violation of the Fifth Amendment, (2) calling into question the prior decisions that were predicated on the proposition that a *Miranda* violation is not the same as a constitutional violation, and (3) excising from the United States Reports a mountain of statements describing the *Miranda* rules as prophylactic.

Subsequent cases confirm that *Dickerson* did not upend the Court's understanding of the *Miranda* rules as prophylactic. In sum, a violation of *Miranda* does not necessarily constitute a violation of the Constitution, and therefore such a violation does not constitute "the deprivation of [a] right . . . secured by the Constitution."

III

This conclusion does not necessarily dictate reversal because a §1983 claim may also be based on "the deprivation of any rights, privileges, or immunities secured by the . . . *laws*." It may thus be argued that the *Miranda* rules constitute federal "law" and that an abridgment of those rules can therefore provide the ground for a §1983 claim. But whatever else may be said about this argument, it cannot succeed unless Tekoh can persuade us that this "law" should be expanded to include the right to sue for damages under §1983.

As we have noted, "[a] judicially crafted" prophylactic rule should apply "only where its benefits outweigh its costs," and here, while the benefits of permitting the assertion of *Miranda* claims under §1983 would be slight, the costs would be substantial.

Miranda rests on a pragmatic judgment about what is needed to stop the violation at trial of the Fifth Amendment right against compelled self-incrimination. That prophylactic purpose is served by the suppression at trial of statements obtained in violation of *Miranda* and by the application of that decision in other recognized contexts. Allowing the victim of a *Miranda* violation to sue a police officer for damages under §1983 would have little additional deterrent value, and permitting such claims would cause many problems.

Allowing a claim like Tekoh's would disserve "judicial economy," by requiring a federal judge or jury to adjudicate a factual question (whether Tekoh was in custody when questioned) that had already been decided by a state court. This re-adjudication would not only be wasteful; it would undercut the "'strong judicial policy against the creation of two conflicting resolutions'" based on the same set of facts. And it could produce "unnecessary friction" between the federal and state court systems by requiring the federal court entertaining the §1983 claim to pass judgment on legal and factual issues already settled in state court.

Allowing §1983 suits based on *Miranda* claims could also present many procedural issues, such as whether a federal court considering a §1983 claim would owe any deference to a trial court's factual findings; whether forfeiture and plain error rules carry over from the criminal trial; whether harmless-error rules apply; and whether civil damages are available in instances where the unwarned statement had no impact on the outcome of the criminal case.

We therefore refuse to extend *Miranda* in the way Tekoh requests. *Miranda*, *Dickerson*, and the other cases in that line provide sufficient protection for the Fifth Amendment right against compelled self-incrimination. "The identification of a *Miranda* violation and its consequences . . . ought to be determined at trial." And except in unusual circumstances, the "exclusion of unwarned statements" should be "a complete and sufficient remedy."

Because a violation of *Miranda* is not itself a violation of the Fifth Amendment, and because we see no justification for expanding *Miranda* to confer a right to sue under §1983, the judgment of the Court of Appeals is reversed, and the case is remanded for further proceedings consistent with this opinion.

Justice KAGAN, with whom Justice BREYER and Justice SOTOMAYOR join, dissenting.

The Court's decision in *Miranda v. Arizona* (1966), affords well-known protections to suspects who are interrogated by police while in custody. Those protections derive from the Constitution: *Dickerson v. United States* tells us in no uncertain terms that *Miranda* is a "constitutional rule." And that rule grants a corresponding right: If police fail to provide the *Miranda* warnings to a suspect before interrogating him, then he is generally entitled to have any resulting confession excluded from his trial. From those facts, only one conclusion can follow—that *Miranda*'s protections are a "right[ ]" "secured by the Constitution" under the federal civil rights statute. 42 U.S.C. §1983. Yet the Court today says otherwise. It holds that *Miranda* is not a constitutional right enforceable through a §1983 suit. And so it prevents individuals from obtaining any redress when police violate their rights under *Miranda*. I respectfully dissent.

Miranda responded to problems stemming from the interrogation of suspects "incommunicado" and "in a police-dominated atmosphere." In such an environment, *Miranda* said, there are "pressures" which may "compel [a suspect] to speak where he would not otherwise do so freely." And so *Miranda* found a "necessity for procedures which assure that the individual is accorded his" Fifth Amendment privilege "not to be compelled to incriminate himself." *Miranda* set out protocols (including the now-familiar warnings) that would safeguard the constitutional privilege against self-incrimination. And *Miranda* held that if police failed to follow those requirements (without substituting equally effective ones), the prosecution could not use at trial a statement obtained from the interrogation.

The question in this case is whether *Miranda*'s protections are a "right[ ]" that is "secured by the Constitution" within the meaning of §1983. If the answer is yes, then a person may sue a state actor who deprives him of the right. In past cases, the Court has given a broad construction to §1983's broad language. Under §1983 (as elsewhere), a "right[ ]" is anything that creates specific "obligations binding on [a] governmental unit" that an individual may ask the judiciary to enforce. And the phrase "secured by the Constitution" also has a capacious meaning. It refers to any right that is "protect[ed] or ma[de] certain" by the country's foundational charter.

Begin with whether *Miranda* is "secured by the Constitution." We know that it is, because the Court's decision in *Dickerson* says so. *Dickerson* tells us again and again that *Miranda* is a "constitutional rule." It is a "constitutional decision" that sets forth "'concrete constitutional guidelines.'" *Miranda* "is constitutionally based"; or again, it has a "constitutional basis." It is "of constitutional origin"; it has "constitutional underpinnings." And—one more—*Miranda* sets a "constitutional minimum." Over and over, *Dickerson* labels *Miranda* a rule stemming from the Constitution.

Dickerson also makes plain that *Miranda* has all the substance of a constitutional rule—including that it cannot be "abrogate[d]" by any "legislation." In *Dickerson*, the Court considered a federal statute whose obvious purpose was to override *Miranda*. *Dickerson* held that *Miranda* is a "constitutional decision" that cannot be "overruled by" any "Act of Congress." To be sure, Congress may devise "legislative solutions that differ[ ] from the prescribed *Miranda* warnings," but only if those solutions are "'at least as effective.'" *Dickerson* therefore instructs (as noted above) that *Miranda* sets a "constitutional minimum." No statute may provide lesser protection than that baseline.

And *Dickerson* makes clear that the constitutional substance of *Miranda* does not end there. Rules arising from "the United States Constitution" are applicable in state-court proceedings, but non-constitutional rules are not. Too, constitutional rules are enforceable in federal-court habeas proceedings, where a prisoner is entitled to claim he "is in custody in violation of the Constitution." *Miranda* checks both boxes. The Court has "consistently applied *Miranda*'s rule to prosecutions arising in state courts." And prisoners may claim *Miranda* violations in federal-court habeas proceedings. So *Dickerson* is unequivocal: *Miranda* is set in constitutional stone.

Miranda's constitutional rule gives suspects a correlative "right[ ]." Under *Miranda*, a suspect typically has a right to be tried without the prosecutor using his un-*Mirandized* statement. And we know how that right operates in the real world. Suppose a defendant standing trial was able to show the court that he gave an un-*Mirandized* confession during a custodial interrogation. The court would have no choice but to exclude it from the prosecutor's case. As one judge below put it: "*Miranda* indisputably creates individual legal rights that are judicially enforceable. (Any prosecutor who doubts this can try to introduce an un-*Mirandized* confession and then watch what happens.)"

The majority basically agrees with everything I've just explained. It concurs that, per *Dickerson*, *Miranda* "adopted a 'constitutional rule.'" How could it not? That *Miranda* is a constitutional rule is what *Dickerson* said (and said and said). The majority also agrees that *Miranda* "directed that statements obtained in violation of [its] rules may not be used by the prosecution in its case-in-chief"—which is simply another way of saying that *Miranda* grants suspects a right to the exclusion of those statements from the prosecutor's case. So how does the majority hold that a violation of *Miranda* is not a "deprivation of [a] right[ ]" "secured by the Constitution"? How does it agree with my premises, but not my conclusion? The majority's argument is that "a violation of *Miranda* does not necessarily constitute a violation of the Constitution," because *Miranda*'s rules are "prophylactic." The idea is that the Fifth Amendment prohibits the use only of statements obtained by compulsion, whereas *Miranda* excludes non-compelled statements too. That is why, the majority says, the Court has been able to recognize exceptions permitting certain uses of un-*Mirandized* statements at trial (when it could not do so for compelled statements).

But none of that helps the majority's case. Let's assume, as the majority says, that *Miranda* extends beyond—in order to safeguard—the Fifth Amendment's core guarantee. Still, *Miranda* is enforceable through §1983. It remains a constitutional rule, as *Dickerson* held (and the majority agrees). And it grants the defendant a legally enforceable entitlement—in a word, a right—to have his confession excluded. So, to refer back to the language of §1983, *Miranda* grants a "right[ ]" "secured by the Constitution." Whether that right to have evidence excluded safeguards a yet deeper constitutional commitment makes no difference to §1983. The majority has no response to that point—except to repeat what our argument assumes already.

Today, the Court strips individuals of the ability to seek a remedy for violations of the right recognized in *Miranda*. The majority observes that defendants may still seek "the suppression at trial of statements obtained" in violation of *Miranda*'s procedures. But sometimes, such a statement will not be suppressed. And sometimes, as a result, a defendant will be wrongly convicted and spend years in prison. He may succeed, on appeal or in habeas, in getting the conviction reversed. But then, what remedy does he have for all the harm he has suffered? The point of §1983 is to provide such redress—because a remedy "is a vital component of any scheme for vindicating cherished constitutional guarantees." The majority here, as elsewhere, injures the right by denying the remedy. I respectfully dissent.

Chapter 9

PLEA BARGAINING AND GUILTY PLEAS

G. Impact of Guilty Pleas (casebook p. 934)

Generally, a guilty plea waives a defendant's right to challenge pretrial issues, including search and seizure violations. However, in *Class v. United States* (2018), the Supreme Court held that, in limited circumstances, a guilty plea does not bar a subsequent constitutional challenge to the statute of conviction.

Class v. United States
138 S. Ct. 798 (2018)

Justice BREYER delivered the opinion of the Court.

Does a guilty plea bar a criminal defendant from later appealing his conviction on the ground that the statute of conviction violates the Constitution? In our view, a guilty plea by itself does not bar that appeal.

I

In September 2013, a federal grand jury indicted petitioner, Rodney Class, for possessing firearms in his locked jeep, which was parked in a lot on the grounds of the United States Capitol in Washington, D.C. Class alleged that the statute, §5104(e), violates the Second Amendment. He also raised a due process claim, arguing that he was denied fair notice that weapons were banned in the parking lot. Following a hearing, the District Court denied both claims.

Several months later, Class pleaded guilty to "Possession of a Firearm on U.S. Capitol Grounds, in violation of 40 U.S.C. §5104(e)." The Government agreed to drop related charges.

A written plea agreement set forth the terms of Class' guilty plea, including several categories of rights that he expressly agreed to waive. At the same time, the plea agreement expressly enumerated categories of claims that Class could raise on appeal. The agreement said nothing about the right to raise on direct appeal a claim that the statute of conviction was unconstitutional.

Class appealed his conviction. He repeated his constitutional claims, namely, that the statute violates the Second Amendment and the Due Process Clause because it fails to give fair notice of which areas fall within the Capitol Grounds where firearms are banned. The Court of Appeals held that Class could not raise his constitutional claims because, by pleading guilty, he had waived them.

II

The question is whether a guilty plea by itself bars a federal criminal defendant from challenging the constitutionality of the statute of conviction on direct appeal. We hold that it does not. Class did not relinquish his right to appeal the District Court's constitutional determinations simply by pleading guilty.

Fifty years ago this Court directly addressed a similar claim (a claim that the statute of conviction was unconstitutional). And the Court stated that a defendant's "plea of guilty did not . . . waive his previous [constitutional] claim." *Haynes v. United States* (1968). Though Justice Harlan's opinion for the Court in *Haynes* offered little explanation for this statement, subsequent decisions offered a rationale that applies here.

In *Blackledge v. Perry* (1974), North Carolina indicted and convicted Jimmy Seth Perry on a misdemeanor assault charge. When Perry exercised his right under a North Carolina statute to a *de novo* trial in a higher court, the State reindicted him, but this time the State charged a felony, which carried a heavier penalty, for the same conduct. Perry pleaded guilty. He then sought habeas relief on the grounds that the reindictment amounted to an unconstitutional vindictive prosecution. The State argued that Perry's guilty plea barred him from raising his constitutional challenge. But this Court held that it did not.

A year and a half later, in *Menna v. New York* (1975), this Court repeated what it had said and held in *Blackledge*. The Court held that "a plea of guilty to a charge does not waive a claim that—judged on its face—the charge is one which the State may not constitutionally prosecute."

These holdings reflect an understanding of the nature of guilty pleas which, in broad outline, stretches back nearly 150 years:

> "The plea of guilty is, of course, a confession of all the facts charged in the indictment, and also of the evil intent imputed to the defendant. It is a waiver also of all merely technical and formal objections of which the defendant could have availed himself by any other plea or motion. But if the facts alleged and admitted do not constitute a crime against the laws of the Commonwealth, the defendant is entitled to be discharged."

Decisions of federal and state courts throughout the 19th and 20th centuries reflect a similar view of the nature of a guilty plea.

[T]he claims at issue here do not fall within any of the categories of claims that Class' plea agreement forbids him to raise on direct appeal. They challenge the Government's power to criminalize Class' (admitted) conduct. They thereby call into question the Government's power to "constitutionally prosecute" him. . . . A guilty plea does not bar a direct appeal in these circumstances.

Justice ALITO, with whom Justice KENNEDY and Justice THOMAS join, dissenting.

9.   Plea Bargaining and Guilty Pleas

Roughly 95% of felony cases in the federal and state courts are resolved by guilty pleas. Therefore it is critically important that defendants, prosecutors, and judges understand the consequences of these pleas. In this case, the parties have asked us to identify the claims that a defendant can raise on appeal after entering an unconditional guilty plea. Regrettably, the Court provides no clear answer.

Blackledge and *Menna* represented marked departures from our prior decisions. Before they were handed down, our precedents were clear: When a defendant pleaded guilty to a crime, he relinquished his right to litigate all nonjurisdictional challenges to his conviction (except for the claim that his plea was not voluntary and intelligent), and the prosecution could assert this forfeiture to defeat a subsequent appeal.

On the strength of that rule, we held that defendants who pleaded guilty forfeited a variety of important constitutional claims. For instance, a defendant who pleaded guilty could not attack his conviction on the ground that the prosecution violated the Equal Protection Clause by systematically excluding African–Americans from grand juries in the county where he was indicted. Nor could he argue that the prosecution unlawfully coerced his confession — even if the confession was the only evidence supporting the conviction. Nor could he assert that his statute of conviction employed an unconstitutional penalty provision; his consent to be punished under the statute precluded this defense.

Blackledge and *Menna* diverged from these prior precedents, but neither case provided a clear or coherent explanation for the departure.

* * *

[T]he governing law in the present case is Rule 11 of the Federal Rules of Criminal Procedure. Under that rule, an unconditional guilty plea waives all nonjurisdictional claims with the possible exception of the *"Menna-Blackledge* doctrine" created years ago by this Court. That doctrine is vacuous, has no sound foundation and produces nothing but confusion. At a minimum, I would limit the doctrine to the particular types of claims involved in those cases. I certainly would not expand its reach.

I fear that today's decision will bedevil the lower courts. I respectfully dissent.

Chapter 11

RIGHT TO COUNSEL

D. Standard for "Effective Assistance" of Counsel (casebook p. 981, after *Strickland v. Washington*)

While great deference is given to defense counsel's strategy, the Supreme Court overturned a death penalty sentence in *Andrus v. Texas* because of defense counsel's failure to provide adequate representation.

Andrus v. Texas

140 S. Ct. 1875 (2020)

Per Curiam

Death-sentenced petitioner Terence Andrus was six years old when his mother began selling drugs out of the apartment where Andrus and his four siblings lived. To fund a spiraling drug addiction, Andrus' mother also turned to prostitution. By the time Andrus was 12, his mother regularly spent entire weekends, at times weeks, away from her five children to binge on drugs. When she did spend time around her children, she often was high and brought with her a revolving door of drug-addicted, sometimes physically violent, boyfriends. Before he reached adolescence, Andrus took on the role of caretaker for his four siblings.

When Andrus was 16, he allegedly served as a lookout while his friends robbed a woman. He was sent to a juvenile detention facility where, for 18 months, he was steeped in gang culture, dosed on high quantities of psychotropic drugs, and frequently relegated to extended stints of solitary confinement. The ordeal left an already traumatized Andrus all but suicidal. Those suicidal urges resurfaced later in Andrus' adult life.

During Andrus' capital trial, however, nearly none of this mitigating evidence reached the jury. That is because Andrus' defense counsel not only neglected to present it; he failed even to look for it. Indeed, counsel performed virtually no investigation of the relevant evidence. Those failures also fettered the defense's capacity to contextualize or counter the State's evidence of Andrus' alleged incidences of past violence.

Only years later, during an 8-day evidentiary hearing in Andrus' state habeas proceeding, did the grim facts of Andrus' life history come to light. And when pressed at the hearing to provide his reasons for failing to investigate Andrus' history, Andrus' counsel offered none.

We conclude that the record makes clear that Andrus has demonstrated counsel's deficient performance under *Strickland*.

I

A

In 2008, 20-year-old Terence Andrus unsuccessfully attempted a carjacking in a grocery-store parking lot while under the influence of PCP-laced marijuana. During the bungled attempt, Andrus fired multiple shots, killing car owner Avelino Diaz and bystander Kim-Phuong Vu Bui. The State charged Andrus with capital murder.

At the guilt phase of trial, Andrus' defense counsel declined to present an opening statement. After the State rested its case, the defense immediately rested as well. In his closing argument, defense counsel conceded Andrus' guilt and informed the jury that the trial would "boil down to the punishment phase," emphasizing that "that's where we are going to be fighting." The jury found Andrus guilty of capital murder.

Trial then turned to the punishment phase. Once again, Andrus' counsel presented no opening statement. In its 3-day case in aggravation, the State put forth evidence that Andrus had displayed aggressive and hostile behavior while confined in a juvenile detention center; that Andrus had tattoos indicating gang affiliations; and that Andrus had hit, kicked, and thrown excrement at prison officials while awaiting trial. The State also presented evidence tying Andrus to an aggravated robbery of a dry-cleaning business. Counsel raised no material objections to the State's evidence and cross-examined the State's witnesses only briefly.

When it came to the defense's case in mitigation, counsel first called Andrus' mother to testify. The direct examination focused on Andrus' basic biographical information and did not reveal any difficult circumstances in Andrus' childhood. Andrus' mother testified that Andrus had an "excellent" relationship with his siblings and grandparents. She also insisted that Andrus "didn't have access to" "drugs or pills in [her] household," and that she would have "counsel[ed] him" had she found out that he was using drugs.

The second witness was Andrus' biological father, Michael Davis, with whom Andrus had lived for about a year when Andrus was around 15 years old. Davis had been in and out of prison for much of Andrus' life and, before he appeared to testify, had not seen Andrus in more than six years. The bulk of Davis' direct examination explored such topics as Davis' criminal history and his relationship with Andrus' mother. Toward the end of the direct examination, counsel elicited testimony that Andrus had been "good around [Davis]" during the 1-year period he had lived with Davis.

Once Davis stepped down, Andrus' counsel informed the court that the defense rested its case and did not intend to call any more witnesses. After the court questioned counsel about this choice during a sidebar discussion, however, counsel changed his mind and decided to call additional witnesses.

11. Right to Counsel

Following a court recess, Andrus' counsel called Dr. John Roache as the defense's only expert witness. Counsel's terse direct examination focused on the general effects of drug use on developing adolescent brains. On cross-examination, the State quizzed Dr. Roache about the relevance and purpose of his testimony, probing pointedly whether Dr. Roache "drove three hours from San Antonio to tell the jury . . . that people change their behavior when they use drugs."

Counsel next called James Martins, a prison counselor who had worked with Andrus. Martins testified that Andrus "started having remorse" in the past two months and was "making progress." *Id.*, at 35. On cross-examination, the State emphasized that Andrus' feelings of remorse had manifested only recently, around the time trial began.

Finally, Andrus himself testified. Contrary to his mother's depiction of his upbringing, he stated that his mother had started selling drugs when he was around six years old, and that he and his siblings were often home alone when they were growing up. He also explained that he first started using drugs regularly around the time he was 15. All told, counsel's questioning about Andrus' childhood comprised four pages of the trial transcript. The State on cross declared, "I have not heard one mitigating circumstance in your life." *Id.*, at 60.

The jury sentenced Andrus to death.

B

After an unsuccessful direct appeal, Andrus filed a state habeas application, principally alleging that his trial counsel was ineffective for failing to investigate or present available mitigation evidence. During an 8-day evidentiary hearing, Andrus presented what the Texas trial court characterized as a "tidal wave of information . . . with regard to mitigation."

The evidence revealed a childhood marked by extreme neglect and privation, a family environment filled with violence and abuse. Andrus was born into a neighborhood of Houston, Texas, known for its frequent shootings, gang fights, and drug overdoses. Andrus' mother had Andrus, her second of five children, when she was 17. The children's fathers never stayed as part of the family. One of them raped Andrus' younger half sister when she was a child. The others—some physically abusive toward Andrus' mother, all addicted to drugs and carrying criminal histories—constantly flitted in and out of the picture.

Starting when Andrus was young, his mother sold drugs and engaged in prostitution. She often made her drug sales at home, in view of Andrus and his siblings. She also habitually used drugs in front of them, and was high more often than not. In her frequently disoriented state, she would leave her children to fend for themselves. Many times, there was not enough food to eat.

After her boyfriend was killed in a shooting, Andrus' mother became increasingly dependent on drugs and neglectful of her children. As a close family friend attested, Andrus' mother "would occasionally just take a week or a weekend and binge [on drugs]. She would get a room somewhere and just go at it."

With the children often left on their own, Andrus assumed responsibility as the head of the household for his four siblings, including his older brother with special needs. Andrus was around 12 years old at the time. He cleaned for his siblings, put them to bed, cooked breakfast for them, made sure they got ready for school, helped them with their homework, and made them dinner. According to his siblings, Andrus was "a protective older brother" who "kept on to [them] to stay out of trouble." Andrus, by their account, was "very caring and very loving," "liked to make people laugh," and "never liked to see people cry." While attempting to care for his siblings, Andrus struggled with mental-health issues: When he was only 10 or 11, he was diagnosed with affective psychosis.

At age 16, Andrus was sentenced to a juvenile detention center run by the Texas Youth Commission (TYC), for allegedly "serv[ing] as the 'lookout'" while he and his friends robbed a woman of her purse. While in TYC custody, Andrus was prescribed high doses of psychotropic drugs carrying serious adverse side effects. He also spent extended periods in isolation, often for purported infractions like reporting that he had heard voices telling him to do bad things. TYC records on Andrus noted multiple instances of self-harm and threats of suicide. After 18 months in TYC custody, Andrus was transferred to an adult prison facility.

Not long after Andrus' release from prison at age 18, Andrus attempted the fatal carjacking that resulted in his capital convictions. While incarcerated awaiting trial, Andrus tried to commit suicide. He slashed his wrist with a razor blade and used his blood to smear messages on the walls, beseeching the world to "[j]ust let [him] die."

II

To prevail on a Sixth Amendment claim alleging ineffective assistance of counsel, a defendant must show that his counsel's performance was deficient and that his counsel's deficient performance prejudiced him. To show deficiency, a defendant must show that "counsel's representation fell below an objective standard of reasonableness." And to establish prejudice, a defendant must show "that there is a reasonable probability that, but for counsel's unprofessional errors, the result of the proceeding would have been different."

To assess whether counsel exercised objectively reasonable judgment under prevailing professional standards, we first ask "whether the investigation supporting counsel's decision not to introduce mitigating evidence of [Andrus'] background was itself reasonable. Here, plainly not. Although counsel nominally put on a case in mitigation in that counsel in fact called witnesses to the stand after the prosecution rested, the record leaves no doubt that counsel's investigation to support that case was an empty exercise.

To start, counsel was, by his own admissions at the habeas hearing, barely acquainted with the witnesses who testified during the case in mitigation. Counsel acknowledged that the first time he met Andrus' mother was when she was subpoenaed to testify, and the first time he met Andrus' biological father was when he

18

showed up at the courthouse to take the stand. Counsel also admitted that he did not get in touch with the third witness (Dr. Roache) until just before *voir dire*, and became aware of the final witness (Martins) only partway through trial.

Over and over during the habeas hearing, counsel acknowledged that he did not look into or present the myriad tragic circumstances that marked Andrus' life. [C]ounsel performed virtually no investigation, either of the few witnesses he called during the case in mitigation, or of the many circumstances in Andrus' life that could have served as powerful mitigating evidence. The untapped body of mitigating evidence was, as the habeas hearing revealed, simply vast.

No doubt due to counsel's failure to investigate the case in mitigation, much of the so-called mitigating evidence he offered unwittingly aided the State's case in aggravation. Counsel's introduction of seemingly *aggravating* evidence confirms the gaping distance between his performance at trial and objectively reasonable professional judgment.

The testimony elicited from Andrus' mother best illustrates this deficiency. First to testify during the case in mitigation, Andrus' mother sketched a portrait of a tranquil upbringing, during which Andrus got himself into trouble despite his family's best efforts. On her account, Andrus fell into drugs entirely on his own: Drugs were not available at home, Andrus did not use them at home, and she would have intervened had she known about Andrus' drug habits. Andrus, his mother related to the jury, "[k]ind of "just decided he didn't want to do what [she] told him to do."

Even though counsel called Andrus' mother as a defense witness, he was ill-prepared for her testimony. [C]ounsel's uninformed decision to call Andrus' mother ultimately undermined Andrus' own testimony.

Counsel also failed to conduct any independent investigation of the State's case in aggravation, despite ample opportunity to do so. During the case in aggravation, the State's task was to prove to the jury that Andrus presented a future danger to society. To that end, the State emphasized that Andrus had acted aggressively in TYC facilities and in prison while awaiting trial. This evidence principally comprised verbal threats, but also included instances of Andrus' kicking, hitting, and throwing excrement at prison officials when they tried to control him. Had counsel genuinely investigated Andrus' experiences in TYC custody, counsel would have learned that Andrus' behavioral problems there were notably mild, and the harms he sustained severe. Or, with sufficient understanding of the violent environments Andrus inhabited his entire life, counsel could have provided a counternarrative of Andrus' later episodes in prison. But instead, counsel left all of that aggravating evidence untouched at trial—even going so far as to inform the jury that the evidence made it "probabl[e]" that Andrus was "a violent kind of guy."

The State's case in aggravation also highlighted Andrus' alleged commission of a knifepoint robbery at a dry-cleaning business. At the time of the offense, "all [that] the crime victim . . . told the police . . . was that he had been the victim of an assault by a black man." Although Andrus stressed to counsel his innocence of the offense, and although the State had not proceeded with charges, Andrus' counsel did not attempt to exclude or rebut the State's evidence.

That is hardly the work of reasonable counsel.

Having found deficient performance, the question remains whether counsel's deficient performance prejudiced Andrus. According to Andrus, effective counsel would have painted a vividly different tableau of aggravating and mitigating evidence than that presented at trial. . . . We conclude that Andrus has shown deficient performance under the first prong of *Strickland*.

Justice ALITO, with whom Justice THOMAS and Justice GORSUCH join, dissenting.

The Court clears this case off the docket, but it does so on a ground that is hard to take seriously. According to the Court, "[i]t is unclear whether the Court of Criminal Appeals considered *Strickland* prejudice at all." But that reading is squarely contradicted by the opinion of the Court of Criminal Appeals (CCA).

Here is what the record shows. According to Andrus's confession, he left his apartment one evening, "'amped up' on embalming fluid [PCP] mixed with marijuana, cocaine, and beer," and looked for a car to "go joy-riding." In the parking lot of a supermarket, he saw Avelino Diaz drop off his wife, Patty, in front of the store. By his own admission, Andrus approached Diaz's car with a gun drawn, but he abandoned the carjacking attempt when he saw that the car had a stick shift, which he could not drive. Alerted by a store employee, Patty Diaz ran out of the store and found her husband lying by the side of the car with a bullet wound in the back of his head. He was subsequently pronounced dead.

After killing Avelino Diaz, Andrus approached a car with two occupants, whom Andrus described as an "old man and old wom[a]n." Andrus fired three shots into the car. The first went through the open driver's side window and hit the passenger, Kim-Phuong Vu Bui, in the head. As the car sped away, Andrus fired a second shot, which entered the back driver's side window, and a third shot, which "entered at an angle indicating that the shot originated from a farther distance." One of these bullets hit the driver, Steve Bui, in the back. Seeing that blood was coming out of his wife's mouth, Steve drove her to a hospital and carried her inside, where she died.

These senseless murders in October 2008 were not Andrus's first crimes. In 2004, he was placed on probation for a drug offense, but just two weeks later, he committed an armed robbery. Andrus and two others followed a woman to her parents' home, where they held her at gunpoint and took her purse and gym bag. The woman identified Andrus as the perpetrator who held the gun.

For this offense, Andrus was sent to a juvenile facility where he showed such "'significant assaultive behavior' toward other youths and staff "that he was eventually transferred to an adult facility. Shortly after his release, he again violated his supervisory conditions and was returned to the adult facility.

When he was released again, he committed an armed robbery of a dry-cleaning establishment. Around 7 A.M. one morning, he entered the business and chased the owner, Tuan Tran, to the back. He beat Tran and threatened him with a knife until Tran gave him money. Less than two months after this crime, Andrus murdered Avelino Diaz and Kim-Phuong Vu Bui.

While awaiting trial for those murders, Andrus carried out a reign of terror in jail. He assaulted another detainee, attacked and injured corrections officers, threw urine in an officer's face, repeatedly made explicit threats to kill officers and staff, flooded his cell and threw excrement on the walls, and engaged in other disruptive acts. Also while awaiting trial for murder, he had the words "murder weapon" tattooed on his hands and a smoking gun tattooed on his forearm.

The CCA has already held once that Andrus failed to establish prejudice. I see no good reason why it should be required to revisit the issue.

Chapter 12

TRIAL BY JURY

B. Jury Composition and Selection

2. Selecting the Petit Jury (casebook p. 1039)

Recently, the Supreme Court applied *Batson* to overturn a death penalty conviction in *Flowers v. Mississippi* (2019). Flowers was tried six times. Over the course of his six trials, the prosecutor used his peremptory challenges to strike 41 of 42 prospective black jurors. The Court found that the facts of the case showed ample evidence of a pattern to discriminate against jurors on the basis of their race.

Flowers v. Mississippi
139 S. Ct. 2228 (2019)

Justice KAVANAUGH delivered the opinion of the Court.

In *Batson v. Kentucky* (1986), this Court ruled that a State may not discriminate on the basis of race when exercising peremptory challenges against prospective jurors in a criminal trial.

In 1996, Curtis Flowers allegedly murdered four people in Winona, Mississippi. Flowers is black. He has been tried six separate times before a jury for murder. The same lead prosecutor represented the State in all six trials. In the initial three trials, Flowers was convicted, but the Mississippi Supreme Court reversed each conviction. In the first trial, Flowers was convicted, but the Mississippi Supreme Court reversed the conviction due to "numerous instances of prosecutorial misconduct." In the second trial, the trial court found that the prosecutor discriminated on the basis of race in the peremptory challenge of a black juror. The trial court seated the black juror. Flowers was then convicted, but the Mississippi Supreme Court again reversed the conviction because of prosecutorial misconduct at trial. In the third trial, Flowers was convicted, but the Mississippi Supreme Court yet again reversed the conviction, this time because the court concluded that the prosecutor had again discriminated against black prospective jurors in the jury selection process. The fourth and fifth trials of Flowers ended in mistrials due to hung juries. In his sixth trial, which is the one at issue here, Flowers was convicted. The State struck five of the six black prospective jurors. On appeal, Flowers argued that the State again violated Batson in exercising peremptory strikes against black prospective jurors.

Four critical facts, taken together, require reversal. First, in the six trials combined, the State employed its peremptory challenges to strike 41 of the 42 black prospective jurors that it could have struck. Second, in the most recent trial, the sixth trial, the State exercised peremptory strikes against five of the six black prospective jurors. Third, at the sixth trial, in an apparent effort to find pretextual reasons to strike black prospective jurors, the State engaged in dramatically disparate questioning of black and white prospective jurors. Fourth, the State then struck at least one black prospective juror, Carolyn Wright, who was similarly situated to white prospective jurors who were not struck by the State.

We need not and do not decide that any one of those four facts alone would require reversal. All that we need to decide, and all that we do decide, is that all of the relevant facts and circumstances taken together establish that the trial court committed clear error in concluding that the State's peremptory strike of black prospective juror Carolyn Wright was not "motivated in substantial part by discriminatory intent."

I

The underlying events that gave rise to this case took place in Winona, Mississippi. Winona is a small town in northern Mississippi. The total population of Winona is about 5,000. The town is about 53 percent black and about 46 percent white. In 1996, Bertha Tardy, Robert Golden, Derrick Stewart, and Carmen Rigby were murdered at the Tardy Furniture store in Winona. All four victims worked at the Tardy Furniture store. Three of the four victims were white; one was black. In 1997, the State charged Curtis Flowers with murder. Flowers is black. Since then, Flowers has been tried six separate times for the murders. In each of the first two trials, Flowers was tried for one individual murder. In each subsequent trial, Flowers was tried for all four of the murders together. The same state prosecutor tried Flowers each time. The prosecutor is white.

At Flowers' first trial, 36 prospective jurors—5 black and 31 white—were presented to potentially serve on the jury. The State exercised a total of 12 peremptory strikes, and it used 5 of them to strike the five qualified black prospective jurors. Flowers objected, arguing under *Batson* that the State had exercised its peremptory strikes in a racially discriminatory manner. At the second trial, 30 prospective jurors—5 black and 25 white—were presented to potentially serve on the jury. As in Flowers' first trial, the State again used its strikes against all five black prospective jurors. But this time, the trial court determined that the State's asserted reason for one of the strikes was a pretext for discrimination. Specifically, the trial court determined that one of the State's proffered reasons—that the juror had been inattentive and was nodding off during jury selection—for striking that juror was false, and the trial court therefore sustained Flowers' *Batson* challenge. The jury at Flowers' second trial consisted of 11 white jurors and 1 black juror. The jury convicted Flowers and sentenced him to death.

At Flowers' third trial, 45 prospective jurors—17 black and 28 white—were presented to potentially serve on the jury. One of the black prospective jurors was struck for cause, leaving 16. The State exercised a total of 15 peremptory strikes, and it used all 15 against black prospective jurors. Flowers again argued that the State had used its peremptory strikes in a racially discriminatory manner.

On appeal, the Mississippi Supreme Court yet again reversed. The court's lead opinion stated: "The instant case presents us with as strong a prima facie case of racial discrimination as we have ever seen in the context of a *Batson* challenge."

At Flowers' fourth trial, 36 prospective jurors—16 black and 20 white—were presented to potentially serve on the jury. The State exercised a total of 11 peremptory strikes, and it used all 11 against black prospective jurors.

At the sixth trial, which we consider here, 26 prospective jurors—6 black and 20 white—were presented to potentially serve on the jury. The State exercised a total of six peremptory strikes, and it used five of the six against black prospective jurors, leaving one black juror to sit on the jury.

II

A

Other than voting, serving on a jury is the most substantial opportunity that most citizens have to participate in the democratic process.

Under *Batson*, once a prima facie case of discrimination has been shown by a defendant, the State must provide race-neutral reasons for its peremptory strikes. The trial judge must determine whether the prosecutor's stated reasons were the actual reasons or instead were a pretext for discrimination. Four parts of *Batson* warrant particular emphasis here.

First, the *Batson* Court rejected Swain's insistence that a defendant demonstrate a history of racially discriminatory strikes in order to make out a claim of race discrimination. In the eyes of the Constitution, one racially discriminatory peremptory strike is one too many. For those reasons, the *Batson* Court held that a criminal defendant could show "purposeful discrimination in selection of the petit jury solely on evidence concerning the prosecutor's exercise of peremptory challenges at the defendant's trial."

Second, the *Batson* Court rejected Swain's statement that a prosecutor could strike a black juror based on an assumption or belief that the black juror would favor a black defendant. In some of the most critical sentences in the Batson opinion, the Court emphasized that a prosecutor may not rebut a claim of discrimination "by stating merely that he challenged jurors of the defendant's race on the assumption—or his intuitive judgment—that they would be partial to the defendant because of their shared race."

Third, the *Batson* Court did not accept the argument that race-based peremptories should be permissible because black, white, Asian, and Hispanic defendants and jurors were all "equally" subject to race-based discrimination.

Fourth, the *Batson* Court did not accept the argument that race-based peremptories are permissible because both the prosecution and defense could employ them in any individual case and in essence balance things out.

B

Equal justice under law requires a criminal trial free of racial discrimination in the jury selection process. Enforcing that constitutional principle, *Batson* ended the widespread practice in which prosecutors could (and often would) routinely strike all black prospective jurors in cases involving black defendants. By taking steps to eradicate racial discrimination from the jury selection process, *Batson* sought to protect the rights of defendants and jurors, and to enhance public confidence in the fairness of the criminal justice system. *Batson* immediately revolutionized the jury selection process that takes place every day in federal and state criminal courtrooms throughout the United States.

In the decades since *Batson*, this Court's cases have vigorously enforced and reinforced the decision, and guarded against any backsliding. Our precedents allow criminal defendants raising Batson challenges to present a variety of evidence to support a claim that a prosecutor's peremptory strikes were made on the basis of race. For example, defendants may present:

- statistical evidence about the prosecutor's use of peremptory strikes against black prospective jurors as compared to white prospective jurors in the case;
- evidence of a prosecutor's disparate questioning and investigation of black and white prospective jurors in the case;
- side-by-side comparisons of black prospective jurors who were struck and white prospective jurors who were not struck in the case;
- a prosecutor's misrepresentations of the record when defending the strikes during the Batson hearing;
- relevant history of the State's peremptory strikes in past cases; or
- other relevant circumstances that bear upon the issue of racial discrimination.

As the *Batson* Court explained and as the Court later reiterated, once a prima facie case of racial discrimination has been established, the prosecutor must provide race-neutral reasons for the strikes. The trial court must consider the prosecutor's race-neutral explanations in light of all of the relevant facts and circumstances, and in light of the arguments of the parties.

An appeals court looks at the same factors as the trial judge, but is necessarily doing so on a paper record. "Since the trial judge's findings in the context under consideration here largely will turn on evaluation of credibility, a reviewing court ordinarily should give those findings great deference."

III

In accord with the principles set forth in *Batson*, we now address Flowers' case.

12. Trial by Jury

The Constitution forbids striking even a single prospective juror for a discriminatory purpose. The question for this Court is whether the Mississippi trial court clearly erred in concluding that the State was not "motivated in substantial part by discriminatory intent" when exercising peremptory strikes at Flowers' sixth trial.

First, we consider the relevant history of the case. Here, our review of the history of the prosecutor's peremptory strikes in Flowers' first four trials strongly supports the conclusion that his use of peremptory strikes in Flowers' sixth trial was motivated in substantial part by discriminatory intent. (Recall that there is no record evidence from the fifth trial regarding the race of the prospective jurors.)

The numbers speak loudly. Over the course of the first four trials, there were 36 black prospective jurors against whom the State could have exercised a peremptory strike. The State tried to strike all 36. Not only did the State's use of peremptory strikes in Flowers' first four trials reveal a blatant pattern of striking black prospective jurors, the Mississippi courts themselves concluded on two separate occasions that the State violated *Batson*. Stretching across Flowers' first four trials, the State employed its peremptory strikes to remove as many black prospective jurors as possible.

We turn now to the State's strikes of five of the six black prospective jurors at Flowers' sixth trial, the trial at issue here. The State's use of peremptory strikes in Flowers' sixth trial followed the same pattern as the first four trials, with one modest exception: It is true that the State accepted one black juror for Flowers' sixth trial. But especially given the history of the case, that fact alone cannot insulate the State from a *Batson* challenge. In *Miller-El II*, this Court skeptically viewed the State's decision to accept one black juror, explaining that a prosecutor might do so in an attempt "to obscure the otherwise consistent pattern of opposition to" seating black jurors. The overall record of this case suggests that the same tactic may have been employed here.

We next consider the State's dramatically disparate questioning of black and white prospective jurors in the jury selection process for Flowers' sixth trial. One can slice and dice the statistics and come up with all sorts of ways to compare the State's questioning of excluded black jurors with the State's questioning of the accepted white jurors. But any meaningful comparison yields the same basic assessment: The State spent far more time questioning the black prospective jurors than the accepted white jurors.

Why did the State ask so many more questions—and conduct more vigorous inquiry—of black prospective jurors than it did of white prospective jurors? No one can know for certain. But this Court's cases explain that disparate questioning and investigation of prospective jurors on the basis of race can arm a prosecutor with seemingly race-neutral reasons to strike the prospective jurors of a particular race. *See Miller-El I*. In other words, by asking a lot of questions of the black prospective jurors or conducting additional inquiry into their backgrounds, a prosecutor can try to find some pretextual reason—any reason—that the prosecutor can later articulate to justify what is in reality a racially motivated strike. And by not doing the same for white prospective jurors, by not asking white prospective jurors those same questions, the prosecutor can try to distort the record so as to thereby avoid being accused of treating black and white jurors differently.

A court confronting that kind of pattern cannot ignore it. The lopsidedness of the prosecutor's questioning and inquiry can itself be evidence of the prosecutor's objective as much as it is of the actual qualifications of the black and white prospective jurors who are struck or seated. The prosecutor's dramatically disparate questioning of black and white prospective jurors—at least if it rises to a certain level of disparity—can supply a clue that the prosecutor may have been seeking to paper the record and disguise a discriminatory intent.

To be clear, disparate questioning or investigation alone does not constitute a *Batson* violation. The disparate questioning or investigation of black and white prospective jurors may reflect ordinary race-neutral considerations. But the disparate questioning or investigation can also, along with other evidence, inform the trial court's evaluation of whether discrimination occurred.

Finally, in combination with the other facts and circumstances in this case, the record of jury selection at the sixth trial shows that the peremptory strike of at least one of the black prospective jurors (Carolyn Wright) was motivated in substantial part by discriminatory intent. In this case, Carolyn Wright was a black prospective juror who said she was strongly in favor of the death penalty as a general matter. And she had a family member who was a prison security guard. Yet the State exercised a peremptory strike against Wright. The State said it struck Wright in part because she knew several defense witnesses and had worked at Wal-Mart where Flowers' father also worked.

Winona is a small town. Wright had some sort of connection to 34 people involved in Flowers' case, both on the prosecution witness side and the defense witness side. But three white prospective jurors—Pamela Chesteen, Harold Waller, and Bobby Lester—also knew many individuals involved in the case. Yet as we explained above, the State did not ask Chesteen, Waller, and Lester individual follow-up questions about their connections to witnesses.

To be sure, the back and forth of a Batson hearing can be hurried, and prosecutors can make mistakes when providing explanations. That is entirely understandable, and mistaken explanations should not be confused with racial discrimination. But when considered with other evidence of discrimination, a series of factually inaccurate explanations for striking black prospective jurors can be telling. So it is here. To reiterate, we need not and do not decide that any one of those four facts alone would require reversal. All that we need to decide, and all that we do decide, is that all of the relevant facts and circumstances taken together establish that the trial court at Flowers' sixth trial committed clear error in concluding that the State's peremptory strike of black prospective juror Carolyn Wright was not motivated in substantial part by discriminatory intent. In reaching that conclusion, we break no new legal ground. We simply enforce and reinforce Batson by applying it to the extraordinary facts of this case.

Justice ALITO, concurring.

As the Court takes pains to note, this is a highly unusual case. In light of all that had gone before, it was risky for the case to be tried once again by the same prosecutor in Montgomery County. Were it not for the unique combinations of circumstances present here, I would have no trouble affirming the decision of the Supreme Court of Mississippi, which conscientiously applied the legal standards applicable in less unusual cases. But viewing the totality of the circumstances present here, I agree with the Court that petitioner's capital conviction cannot stand.

Justice THOMAS, with whom Justice GORSUCH joins as to Parts I, II, and III, dissenting.[1]

The Court today does not dispute that the evidence was sufficient to convict Flowers or that he was tried by an impartial jury. Instead, the Court vacates Flowers' convictions on the ground that the state courts clearly erred in finding that the State did not discriminate based on race when it struck Carolyn Wright from the jury.

The only clear errors in this case are committed by today's majority. Today's decision distorts the record of this case, eviscerates our standard of review, and vacates four murder convictions because the State struck a juror who would have been stricken by any competent attorney. I dissent.

If this case required us to decide whether the state courts were correct that no Batson violation occurred here, I would find the case easy enough. As I have demonstrated, the evidence overwhelmingly supports the conclusion that the State did not engage in purposeful race discrimination. Any competent prosecutor would have struck the jurors struck below. Indeed, some of the jurors' conflicts might even have justified for-cause strikes. But this case is easier yet. The question before us is not whether we "'would have decided the case differently,'" but instead whether the state courts were clearly wrong. And the answer to that question is obviously no.

Much of the Court's opinion is a paean to *Batson v. Kentucky*, which requires that a duly convicted criminal go free because a juror was arguably deprived of his right to serve on the jury. That rule was suspect when it was announced, and I am even less confident of it today.

Flowers should not have standing to assert the excluded juror's claim. He does not dispute that the jury that convicted him was impartial, and as the Court has said many times. He therefore suffered no legally cognizable injury.

Today, the Court holds that Carolyn Wright was denied equal protection by being excluded from jury service. But she is not the person challenging Flowers' convictions (she would lack standing to do so), and I do not understand how Flowers can have standing to assert her claim. The "entire line of cases following

[1] Editor's Note: In Part IV of his dissent, Justice Thomas challenges the ongoing validity of *Batson v. Kentucky*.

Batson" is "a misguided effort to remedy a general societal wrong by using the Constitution to regulate the traditionally discretionary exercise of peremptory challenges."

C.   Pretrial Publicity and the Right to a Fair Trial

1.   When Does Pretrial Publicity Interfere with a Defendant's Right to a Fair Trial? (casebook p. 1061)

Most recently, the Supreme Court has held that trial judges should be granted great deference in how they conduct the jury-selection process, including in cases involving a high degree of pretrial publicity.

United States v. Tsarnaev
142 S. Ct. 1024 (2022)

Justice THOMAS delivered the opinion of the Court.

On April 15, 2013, Dzhokhar and Tamerlan Tsarnaev planted and detonated two homemade pressure-cooker bombs near the finish line of the Boston Marathon. The blasts hurled nails and metal debris into the assembled crowd, killing three while maiming and wounding hundreds. Three days later, the brothers murdered a campus police officer, carjacked a graduate student, and fired on police who had located them in the stolen vehicle. Dzhokhar attempted to flee in the vehicle but inadvertently killed Tamerlan by running him over. Dzhokhar was soon arrested and indicted.

A jury found Dzhokhar guilty of 30 federal crimes and recommended the death penalty for 6 of them. The District Court accordingly sentenced Dzhokhar to death. The Court of Appeals vacated the death sentence. We now reverse.[2]

I

A

The Tsarnaev brothers immigrated to the United States in the early 2000s and lived in Massachusetts. Little more than a decade later, they were actively contemplating how to wage radical jihad. They downloaded and read al Qaeda propaganda, and, by December of 2012, began studying an al Qaeda guide to bomb making.

---

[2] The Court of Appeals reversed the death sentence on two grounds. The first ground related to the jury selection process; the second ground related to proffered mitigating evidence for the penalty phase of the trial. This redacted decision addresses only the first issue related to pretrial publicity and jury selection. [Footnote by authors.]

12. Trial by Jury

On April 15, 2013, the brothers went to the Boston Marathon finish line on Boylston Street. They each brought a backpack containing a homemade pressure-cooker bomb packed with explosives inside a layer of nails, BBs, and other metal scraps. Tamerlan left his backpack in a crowd of spectators and walked away. Dzhokhar stood with his backpack outside the Forum, a nearby restaurant where spectators watched the runners from the sidewalk and dining patio. For four minutes, Dzhokhar surveyed the crowd. After speaking with Tamerlan by phone, Dzhokhar left his backpack among the spectators. Tamerlan then detonated his bomb. While the crowd at the Forum looked toward the explosion, Dzhokhar walked the other way. After a few seconds, he detonated his bomb.

Each detonation sent fire and shrapnel in all directions. The blast from Tamerlan's bomb shattered Krystle Campbell's left femur and mutilated her legs. Though bystanders tried to save her, she bled to death on the sidewalk. Dzhokhar's bomb ripped open the legs of Boston University student Lingzi Lu. Rescuers tried to stem the bleeding by using a belt as a makeshift tourniquet. She too bled to death.

Eight-year-old Martin Richard absorbed the full blast of Dzhokhar's bomb. BBs, nails, and other metal fragments shot through his abdomen, cutting through his aorta, spinal cord, spleen, liver, pancreas, left kidney, and large intestines. The blast propelled shrapnel with such force that it exited his back. Other shrapnel nearly severed his left hand. The explosion also caused third-degree burns. Martin ultimately died from blood loss.

Dzhokhar's and Tamerlan's bombs maimed and wounded hundreds of other victims. Many people lost limbs, including Martin's 6-year-old sister, Jane. Many more would have died if not for the swift action of citizens and first responders.

B

A federal grand jury indicted Dzhokhar for 30 crimes, 17 of which were capital offenses. In preparation for jury selection, the parties jointly proposed a 100-question form to screen the prospective jurors. The District Court adopted almost all of them, including many that probed for bias. For example, some of the District Court's questions asked whether a prospective juror had a close association with law enforcement. Others asked whether a prospective juror had strong feelings about Islam, Chechens, or the several Central Asian regions with which the Tsarnaevs were connected. Still others asked whether the prospective juror had a personal connection to the bombing.

Several questions also probed whether media coverage might have biased a prospective juror. One question asked if the prospective juror had "formed an opinion" about the case because of what he had "seen or read in the news media." Others asked about the source, amount, and timing of the person's media consumption. Still another asked whether the prospective juror had commented or posted online about the bombings.

The District Court did reject one media-related question. The proposed questionnaire had asked each prospective juror to list the facts he had learned about the case from the media and other sources. Concerned that such a broad, "unfocused" question would "cause trouble" by producing "unmanageable data" of minimal value that would come to dominate the entire *voir dire*, the District Court declined to include it in the questionnaire. After Dzhokhar objected to the removal, the District Court further explained that the question was "too unguided."

Recognizing the intense public interest in the case, the District Court summoned an expanded jury pool. In early January 2015, the court called 1,373 prospective jurors for the first round of jury selection. After reviewing their answers to the questionnaire, the court reduced the pool to 256. As jury selection began in earnest, Dzhokhar renewed his request that the court ask each juror about the content of the media he had consumed. The District Court again refused Dzhokhar's blanket request and instead permitted counsel to ask appropriate followup questions about a prospective juror's media consumption based on the answers to questions in the questionnaire or at *voir dire*. Several times, the court permitted Dzhokhar's attorneys to follow up on a prospective juror's earlier answers with specific questions about what the juror had seen or heard in the news. Over the course of three weeks of in-person questioning, the District Court and the parties reduced the 256 prospective jurors down to 12 seated jurors.

C

The Court of Appeals vacated Dzhokhar's capital sentence on two grounds. First, the Court of Appeals held that the District Court abused its discretion during jury selection by declining to ask every prospective juror what he learned from the media about the case. Second, the panel held that the District Court abused its discretion when it excluded from sentencing. We granted certiorari.

II

The Government argues that the Court of Appeals improperly vacated Dzhokhar's capital sentences based on the juror questionnaire and the Waltham evidence. We agree.

A

The Sixth Amendment guarantees "the accused" the right to a trial "by an impartial jury." The right to an "impartial" jury "does not require *ignorance*." *Skilling v. United States* (2010). Notorious crimes are "almost, as a matter of necessity, brought to the attention" of those informed citizens who are "best fitted" for jury duty. A trial court protects the defendant's Sixth Amendment right by ensuring that jurors have "no bias or prejudice that would prevent them from returning a verdict according to the law and evidence."

We have repeatedly said that jury selection falls "'particularly within the province of the trial judge.'" *Skilling*, 561 U.S., at 386. That is so because a trial "judge's appraisal is ordinarily influenced by a host of factors impossible to capture fully in the record," such as a "prospective juror's inflection, sincerity, demeanor, candor, body language, and apprehension of duty." A trial court's broad discretion in this area includes deciding what questions to ask prospective jurors.

A court of appeals reviews the district court's questioning of prospective jurors only for abuse of discretion. That discretion does not vanish when a case garners public attention. Indeed, "[w]hen pretrial publicity is at issue, 'primary reliance on the judgment of the trial court makes [especially] good sense.'" *Skilling*, 561 U.S., at 386. After all, "the judge 'sits in the locale where the publicity is said to have had its effect' and may base her evaluation on her 'own perception of the depth and extent of news stories that might influence a juror.'" Because conducting *voir dire* is committed to the district court's sound discretion, there is no blanket constitutional requirement that it must ask each prospective juror what he heard, read, or saw about a case in the media. Instead, as in any case, the district court's duty is to conduct a thorough jury-selection process that allows the judge to evaluate whether each prospective juror is "to be believed when he says he has not formed an opinion about the case."

The District Court did not abuse its broad discretion by declining to ask about the content and extent of each juror's media consumption regarding the bombings. The court recognized the significant pretrial publicity concerning the bombings, and reasonably concluded that the proposed media-content question was "unfocused," risked producing "unmanageable data," and would at best shed light on "preconceptions" that other questions already probed. At *voir dire*, the court further explained that it did not want to be "too tied to a script" because "[e]very juror is different" and had to be "questioned in a way that [was] appropriate" to the juror's earlier answers. The court was concerned that a media-content question had "the wrong emphasis," focusing on what a juror knew before coming to court, rather than on potential bias. Based on "years" of trial experience, the court concluded that jurors who came in with some prior knowledge would still be able to act impartially and "hold the government to its proof." The District Court's decision was reasonable and well within its discretion, as our precedents make clear.

If any doubt remained, the rest of the jury-selection process dispels it. The District Court summoned an expanded jury pool of 1,373 prospective jurors and used the 100-question juror form to cull that down to 256. The questionnaire asked prospective jurors what media sources they followed, how much they consumed, whether they had ever commented on the bombings in letters, calls, or online posts, and, most pointedly, whether any of that information had caused the prospective juror to form an opinion about Dzhokhar's guilt or punishment. The court then subjected those 256 prospective jurors to three weeks of individualized *voir dire* in which the court and both parties had the opportunity to ask additional questions and probe for bias. Dzhokhar's attorneys asked several prospective jurors what they had heard, read, or seen about the case in the media. The District Court also provided "'emphatic and clear instructions on the sworn duty of each juror to decide the issues only on evidence presented in open court.'" The court reminded the prospective jurors that they "must be able to decide the issues in the case based on the information or evidence that is presented in the course of the trial, not on information from any other sources," an instruction the court gave during *voir dire* and repeated during the trial. In sum, the court's jury selection process was both eminently reasonable and wholly consistent with this Court's precedents.

The Court of Appeals erred in holding otherwise. As it saw things, its decision nearly 50 years prior in *Patriarca v. United States*, 402 F.2d 314 (1st Cir. 1968) had, pursuant to its "supervisory authority," required district courts presiding over high-profile cases to ask about the "'kind and degree of [the prospective juror's] exposure to the case or the parties.'"

It is true that some of our precedents describe a "supervisory authority" that inheres in federal courts. But the Court's precedents have also identified clear limits when lower courts have purported to invoke that authority. For example, supervisory rules cannot conflict with or circumvent a constitutional provision or federal statute. Finally, and most relevant here, lower courts cannot create prophylactic supervisory rules that circumvent or supplement legal standards set out in decisions of this Court.

This Court has held many times that a district court enjoys broad discretion to manage jury selection, including what questions to ask prospective jurors. As the Court of Appeals acknowledged, our cases establish that a reviewing court may set aside a district court's questioning only for an abuse of discretion. The Court of Appeals declined to apply that settled standard of review. Rather than ask whether media-content questions were necessary in light of the District Court's exhaustive *voir dire*, the Court of Appeals resurrected *Patriarca*, handed down a purported legal rule that media-content questions are required in all high-profile cases, and then concluded that the District Court committed a legal error when it failed to comply with that rule. But a court of appeals cannot supplant the district court's broad discretion to manage *voir dire* by prescribing specific lines of questioning, and thereby circumvent a well-established standard of review. Whatever the "supervisory power" entails, it does not countenance the Court of Appeals' use of it.

III

Dzhokhar Tsarnaev committed heinous crimes. The *Sixth Amendment* nonetheless guaranteed him a fair trial before an impartial jury. He received one. The judgment of the United States Court of Appeals for the First Circuit is reversed.

JUSTICE BREYER, with whom JUSTICE SOTOMAYOR and JUSTICE KAGAN join dissenting.

[The dissent focused exclusively on the second issue in the case and whether Dzhokhar Tsarnaev should have been permitted to introduce evidence regarding his older brother Tamerlan in mitigation of Dzhokhar's role in the bombings].

Chapter 13

SENTENCING

D. The Death Penalty

3. Recent Limits on the Scope of the Death Penalty

d. *Method of Execution* (casebook p. 1225)

In *Glossip v. Gross*, 135 S. Ct. 2726 (2015), the Supreme Court clarified that the plurality opinion in *Baze v. Rees*, 553 U.S. 35 (2008), was controlling. Under *Baze v. Rees* and *Glossip v. Gross*, an inmate challenging a method of execution must demonstrate that there is an alternative form of execution that would not cause the severe pain in the challenged execution method. In *Bucklew v. Precythe* (2019), the condemned inmate failed to make that necessary showing.

Bucklew v. Precythe
139 S. Ct. 1112 (2019)

Justice GORSUCH delivered the opinion of the Court.

Russell Bucklew concedes that the State of Missouri lawfully convicted him of murder and a variety of other crimes. He acknowledges that the U.S. Constitution permits a sentence of execution for his crimes. He accepts, too, that the State's lethal injection protocol is constitutional in most applications. But because of his unusual medical condition, he contends the protocol is unconstitutional as applied to him.

I

A

In 1996, when Stephanie Ray announced that she wanted to end their relationship, Mr. Bucklew grew violent. He cut her jaw, punched her in the face, and threatened her with a knife. Frightened to remain in the home they had shared, Ms. Ray sought refuge with her children in Michael Sanders' nearby residence. But then one night Mr. Bucklew invaded that home. Bearing a pistol in each hand, he shot Mr. Sanders in the chest; fired at Mr. Sanders' 6-year-old son (thankfully, he missed); and pistol-whipped Ms. Ray, this time breaking her jaw. Then Mr. Bucklew handcuffed Ms. Ray, drove her to a secluded spot, and raped her at gunpoint. After a trooper spotted Mr. Bucklew, a shootout followed and he was finally arrested. While all this played out, Mr. Sanders bled to death. As a coda, Mr. Bucklew escaped from jail while awaiting trial and attacked Ms. Ray's mother with a hammer before he could be recaptured.

A jury had convicted him of murder and other crimes and recommended a death sentence, which the court had imposed.

Mr. Bucklew's case soon became caught up in a wave of litigation over lethal injection procedures. Like many States, Missouri has periodically sought to improve its administration of the death penalty. Early in the 20th century, the State replaced hanging with the gas chamber. Later in the century, it authorized the use of lethal injection as an alternative to lethal gas. By the time Mr. Bucklew's post-conviction proceedings ended, Missouri's protocol called for lethal injections to be carried out using three drugs: sodium thiopental, pancuronium bromide, and potassium chloride. And by that time, too, various inmates were in the process of challenging the constitutionality of the State's protocol and others like it around the country.

While all this played out, pressure from anti-death-penalty advocates induced the company that manufactured sodium thiopental to stop supplying it for use in executions. As a result, the State was unable to proceed with executions until it could change its lethal injection protocol again. This it did in 2012, prescribing the use of a single drug, the sedative propofol. Soon after that, Mr. Bucklew and other inmates sued to invalidate this new protocol as well, alleging that it would produce excruciating pain and violate the Eighth Amendment on its face. After the State revised the protocol in 2013 to use the sedative pentobarbital instead of propofol, the inmates amended their complaint to allege that pentobarbital would likewise violate the Constitution.

Things came to a head in 2014. With its new protocol in place and the necessary drugs now available, the State scheduled Mr. Bucklew's execution for May 21. But 12 days before the execution Mr. Bucklew filed yet another lawsuit, the one now before us. In this case, he presented an as-applied Eighth Amendment challenge to the State's new protocol. Whether or not it would cause excruciating pain for all prisoners, as his previous lawsuit alleged, Mr. Bucklew now contended that the State's protocol would cause him severe pain because of his particular medical condition. Mr. Bucklew suffers from a disease called cavernous hemangioma, which causes vascular tumors—clumps of blood vessels—to grow in his head, neck, and throat. His complaint alleged that this condition could prevent the pentobarbital from circulating properly in his body; that the use of a chemical dye to flush the intravenous line could cause his blood pressure to spike and his tumors to rupture; and that pentobarbital could interact adversely with his other medications.

[In] *Glossip v. Gross* (2015), this Court reject[ed] a challenge to Oklahoma's lethal injection protocol. There, the Court clarified that . . . an inmate cannot successfully challenge a method of execution under the Eighth Amendment unless he identifies "an alternative that is 'feasible, readily implemented, and in fact significantly reduces a substantial risk of severe pain.'" Justice Thomas, joined by Justice Scalia, reiterated his view that the Eighth Amendment "prohibits only those methods of execution that are deliberately designed to inflict pain," but he joined the Court's opinion because it correctly explained why petitioners' claim failed even under the controlling opinion in *Baze*.

Despite . . . express instructions, when Mr. Bucklew returned to the district court in 2015 he still refused to identify an alternative procedure that would significantly reduce his alleged risk of pain. Mr. Bucklew's contentions about the pain he might suffer had evolved considerably. He no longer complained about circulation of the drug, the use of dye, or adverse drug interactions. Instead, his main claim now was that he would experience pain during the period after the pentobarbital started to take effect but before it rendered him fully unconscious. According to his expert, Dr. Joel Zivot, while in this semiconscious "twilight stage" Mr. Bucklew would be unable to prevent his tumors from obstructing his breathing, which would make him feel like he was suffocating.

II

We begin with Mr. Bucklew's suggestion that the test for lethal injection protocol challenges announced in *Baze* and *Glossip* should govern only facial challenges, not as-applied challenges like his.

The Constitution allows capital punishment. In fact, death was "the standard penalty for all serious crimes" at the time of the founding. Of course, that doesn't mean the American people must continue to use the death penalty. The same Constitution that permits States to authorize capital punishment also allows them to outlaw it. But it does mean that the judiciary bears no license to end a debate reserved for the people and their representatives.

While the Eighth Amendment doesn't forbid capital punishment, it does speak to how States may carry out that punishment, prohibiting methods that are "cruel and unusual." What does this term mean? At the time of the framing, English law still formally tolerated certain punishments even though they had largely fallen into disuse—punishments in which "terror, pain, or disgrace [were] superadded" to the penalty of death. These included such "[d]isgusting" practices as dragging the prisoner to the place of execution, disemboweling, quartering, public dissection, and burning alive, all of which Blackstone observed "savor[ed] of torture or cruelty."

Methods of execution like these readily qualified as "cruel and unusual." as a reader at the time of the Eighth Amendment's adoption would have understood those words. They were undoubtedly "cruel," a term often defined to mean "[p]leased with hurting others; inhuman; hard-hearted; void of pity; wanting compassion; savage; barbarous; unrelenting,"

Consistent with the Constitution's original understanding, this Court in *Wilkerson v. Utah* (1879), permitted an execution by firing squad while observing that the Eighth Amendment forbade the gruesome methods of execution described by Blackstone "and all others in the same line of unnecessary cruelty." A few years later, the Court upheld a sentence of death by electrocution while observing that, though electrocution was a new mode of punishment and therefore perhaps could be considered "unusual," it was not "cruel" in the constitutional sense.

At the time of the [Eighth] Amendment's adoption, the predominant method of execution in this country was hanging. While hanging was considered more humane than some of the punishments of the Old World, it was no guarantee of a quick and painless death.

What does all this tell us about how the Eighth Amendment applies to methods of execution? For one thing, it tells us that the Eighth Amendment does not guarantee a prisoner a painless death — something that, of course, isn't guaranteed to many people, including most victims of capital crimes. Instead, what unites the punishments the Eighth Amendment was understood to forbid, and distinguishes them from those it was understood to allow, is that the former were long disused (unusual) forms of punishment that intensified the sentence of death with a (cruel) "'superadd[ition]'" of "'terror, pain, or disgrace.'"

This Court has yet to hold that a State's method of execution qualifies as cruel and unusual, and perhaps understandably so. Far from seeking to superadd terror, pain, or disgrace to their executions, the States have often sought more nearly the opposite. Notably, all of these innovations occurred not through this Court's intervention, but through the initiative of the people and their representatives.

III

Having (re)confirmed that anyone bringing a method of execution claim alleging the infliction of unconstitutionally cruel pain must meet the *Baze-Glossip* test, we can now turn to the question whether Mr. Bucklew is able to satisfy that test. Has he identified a feasible and readily implemented alternative method of execution the State refused to adopt without a legitimate reason, even though it would significantly reduce a substantial risk of severe pain? Because the case comes to us after the entry of summary judgment, this appeal turns on whether Mr. Bucklew has shown a genuine issue of material fact warranting a trial.

We begin with the question of a proposed alternative method. Through much of this case and despite many opportunities, Mr. Bucklew refused to identify any alternative method of execution, choosing instead to stand on his argument that *Baze* and *Glossip*'s legal standard doesn't govern as-applied challenges like his (even after the Eighth Circuit rejected that argument). Only when the district court warned that his continued refusal to abide this Court's precedents would result in immediate dismissal did Mr. Bucklew finally point to nitrogen hypoxia. The district court then afforded Mr. Bucklew "extensive discovery" to explore the viability of that alternative. But even after all that, we conclude Mr. Bucklew has failed for two independent reasons to present a triable question on the viability of nitrogen hypoxia as an alternative to the State's lethal injection protocol.

First, an inmate must show that his proposed alternative method is not just theoretically "'feasible'" but also "'readily implemented.'" This means the inmate's proposal must be sufficiently detailed to permit a finding that the State could carry it out "relatively easily and reasonably quickly." Mr. Bucklew's bare-bones proposal falls well short of that standard. He has presented no evidence on essential questions like how nitrogen gas should be administered (using a gas chamber, a tent, a hood, a mask, or some other delivery device); in what concentration (pure nitrogen or some mixture of gases); how quickly and for how long it should be introduced; or how the State might ensure the safety of the execution team, including protecting them against the risk of gas leaks.

Second, and relatedly, the State had a "legitimate" reason for declining to switch from its current method of execution as a matter of law. Rather than point to a proven alternative method, Mr. Bucklew sought the adoption of an entirely new method—one that had "never been used to carry out an execution" and had "no track record of successful use."

Even if a prisoner can carry his burden of showing a readily available alternative, he must still show that it would significantly reduce a substantial risk of severe pain. A minor reduction in risk is insufficient; the difference must be clear and considerable. Over the course of this litigation, Mr. Bucklew's explanation why nitrogen hypoxia meets this standard has evolved significantly. But neither of the two theories he has advanced in this Court turns out to be supported by record evidence.

First, Mr. Bucklew points to several risks that he alleges could result from use of the State's lethal injection protocol that would not be present if the State used nitrogen gas. For example, he says the execution team might try to insert an IV into one of his peripheral veins, which could cause the vein to rupture; or the team might instead use an allegedly painful "cut-down" procedure to access his femoral vein. He also says that he might be forced to lie flat on his back during the execution, which could impair his breathing even before the pentobarbital is administered. And he says the stress from all this could cause his tumors to bleed, further impairing his breathing. These risks, we may assume, would not exist if Mr. Bucklew were executed by his preferred method of nitrogen hypoxia.

The problem with all of these contentions is that they rest on speculation unsupported, if not affirmatively contradicted, by the evidence in this case. . . . In sum, even if execution by nitrogen hypoxia were a feasible and readily implemented alternative to the State's chosen method, Mr. Bucklew has still failed to present any evidence suggesting that it would significantly reduce his risk of pain. For that reason as well, the State was entitled to summary judgment on Mr. Bucklew's Eighth Amendment claim.

IV

"Both the State and the victims of crime have an important interest in the timely enforcement of a sentence." Those interests have been frustrated in this case. Mr. Bucklew committed his crimes more than two decades ago. He exhausted his appeal and separate state and federal habeas challenges more than a decade ago. Yet since then he has managed to secure delay through lawsuit after lawsuit.

The people of Missouri, the surviving victims of Mr. Bucklew's crimes, and others like them deserve better. Last-minute stays should be the extreme exception.

The judgment of the court of appeals is affirmed.

Justice THOMAS, concurring.

I adhere to my view that "a method of execution violates the Eighth Amendment only if it is deliberately designed to inflict pain."

Justice KAVANAUGH, concurring.

When an inmate raises an as-applied constitutional challenge to a particular method of execution—that is, a challenge to a method of execution that is constitutional in general but that the inmate says is very likely to cause him severe pain—one question is whether the inmate must identify an available alternative method of execution that would significantly reduce the risk of severe pain. Applying our recent decisions in *Glossip v. Gross* and *Baze v. Rees*, the Court's answer to that question is yes. Under those precedents, I agree with the Court's holding and join the Court's opinion.

Justice BREYER with whom Justice GINSBURG, Justice SOTOMAYOR, and Justice KAGAN join as to all but Part III, dissenting.

Bucklew has easily established a genuine issue of material fact regarding whether an execution by lethal injection would subject him to impermissible suffering. The record indicates that Bucklew suffers from a congenital condition known as cavernous hemangioma that causes tumors filled with blood vessels to grow throughout his body, including in his head, face, neck, and oral cavity. The condition is rare. One study estimates that hemangiomas in the oral cavity occur in less than one percent of the population, and that hemangiomas like Bucklew's have been identified in five cases.

Tumors grow out of Bucklew's lip and over his mouth, as well as on his hard and soft palates. One tumor also grows directly on Bucklew's uvula, which has become "grossly enlarged" as a result. Bucklew's tumors obstruct his airway and make it difficult for him to breathe. His difficulty breathing is chronic, but is particularly acute when he lies flat and gravity pulls his engorged uvula into his airway. He often has to adjust the positioning of his head to prevent his uvula from obstructing his breathing. He sleeps at a 45-degree angle to facilitate breathing, and he often wakes up in the middle of the night gasping for air.

Due to the sensitivity of his tumors, even minimal contact may cause them to hemorrhage. He has described past hemorrhages as "'squirting'" or "leaking" blood, and he states that the first thing he does each morning is to wipe the blood off his face that leaked from his nose and mouth as he slept. Bucklew's condition is progressive and, due to the risk of significant blood loss caused by the sensitivity of his tumors, cannot be treated by surgery.

Bucklew maintains that, as a result of this medical condition, executing him by lethal injection would prove excruciatingly painful. In support of this claim, Bucklew submitted sworn declarations and deposition testimony from an expert witness, Dr. Joel Zivot, an anesthesiologist. The State asked the District Court to grant summary judgment in its favor on the theory that Bucklew failed to identify a genuine factual issue regarding whether an execution by lethal injection would be impermissibly painful. The District Court refused.

The District Court was right. The evidence, taken in the light most favorable to Bucklew, creates a genuine factual issue as to whether Missouri's lethal injection protocol would subject him to several minutes of "severe pain and suffering,"

I accept the *Glossip* majority opinion as governing. I nonetheless do not believe its "alternative method" requirement applies in this case. [W]hile I acknowledge that the Court in *Glossip* spoke in unqualified terms, the circumstances in *Glossip* were indeed "different" in relevant respects from the circumstances presented here.

The *Glossip* Court, in adopting the "alternative method" requirement, relied on the Chief Justice's plurality opinion in *Baze*, which discussed the need to avoid "intrud[ing] on the role of state legislatures in implementing their execution procedures." But no such intrusion problem exists in a case like this one. When adopting a method of execution, a state legislature will rarely consider the method's application to an individual who, like Bucklew, suffers from a rare disease. It is impossible to believe that Missouri's legislature, when adopting lethal injection, considered the possibility that it would cause prisoners to choke on their own blood for up to several minutes before they die. Exempting a prisoner from the State's chosen method of execution in these circumstances does not interfere with any legislative judgment.

Even assuming for argument's sake that Bucklew must bear the burden of showing the existence of a "known and available" alternative method of execution that "significantly reduces a substantial risk of severe pain," Bucklew has satisfied that burden. Bucklew identified as an alternative method of execution the use of nitrogen hypoxia, which is a form of execution by lethal gas. Missouri law permits the use of this method of execution. Three other States—Alabama, Mississippi, and Oklahoma—have specifically authorized nitrogen hypoxia as a method of execution. Presented with evidence such as Bucklew's, I believe a State should take at least minimal steps to determine the feasibility of the proposed alternative.

Justice Thomas concurs in the majority's imposition of an "alternative method" requirement, but would also permit Bucklew's execution on the theory that a method of execution violates the Eighth Amendment "'only if it is deliberately designed to inflict pain.'" But that is not the proper standard.

Today's majority appears to believe that because "[t]he Constitution allows capital punishment," the Constitution must allow capital punishment to occur quickly. It may be that there is no way to execute a prisoner quickly while affording him the protections that our Constitution guarantees to those who have been singled out for our law's most severe sanction. And it may be that, as our Nation comes to place ever greater importance upon ensuring that we accurately identify, through procedurally fair methods, those who may lawfully be put to death, there simply is no constitutional way to implement the death penalty.

Justice SOTOMAYOR, dissenting.

As I have maintained ever since the Court started down this wayward path in *Glossip v. Gross*, there is no sound basis in the Constitution for requiring condemned inmates to identify an available means for their own executions. I am [also] especially troubled by the majority's statement that "[l]ast-minute stays should be the extreme exception," which could be read to intimate that late-occurring stay requests from capital prisoners should be reviewed with an especially jaundiced eye.

There are higher values than ensuring that executions run on time. If a death sentence or the manner in which it is carried out violates the Constitution, that stain can never come out. Our jurisprudence must remain one of vigilance and care, not one of dismissiveness.

In *Nance v. Ward*, 142 S. Ct. 2214 (2022), the Supreme Court held that a challenge to the method of execution may be made pursuant to an action under 42 U.S.C. §1983.

In addition to addressing the manner of execution, the Supreme Court in *Ramirez v. Collier*, 142 S. Ct. 1264 (2022), held that a categorical ban on a spiritual advisor touching the inmate or reciting an audible prayer during the execution is a violation of the Religious Land Use and Institutionalized Persons Act of 2000 (RLUIPA) and the First Amendment. Restrictions on religious practices during an execution must be the least restrictive means of furthering a state's compelling interest in preventing disruptions in the execution chamber.

Chapter 14

DOUBLE JEOPARDY

D. Exceptions to the Double Jeopardy Rule

2. Dual Sovereignty (casebook p. 1252)

Following the Supreme Court's decision in *Gamble v. United States* (2019), in which the Court reaffirmed the separate sovereign exception to the Double Jeopardy rule, the Supreme decided *Denezpi v. United States*, 142 S. Ct. 395 (June 13, 2022). In *Denezpi*, the Court upheld the prosecution of a defendant twice by federal authorities for the same criminal act—first for violation of Tribal law and then for violation of federal law. The Court held that "[b]ecause the Tribe and the Federal Government are distinct sovereigns, those 'offence[s]' are not 'the same.' Denezpi's second prosecution therefore did not offend the Double Jeopardy Clause."

Denezpi v. United States
142 S. Ct. 395 (2022)

Justice BARRETT delivered the opinion of the Court.

The Double Jeopardy Clause protects a person from being prosecuted twice "for the same offence." An offense defined by one sovereign is necessarily different from an offense defined by another, even when the offenses have identical elements. Thus, a person can be successively prosecuted for the two offenses without offending the Clause. We have dubbed this the "dual-sovereignty" doctrine.

This case presents a twist on the usual dual-sovereignty scenario. The mine run of these cases involves two sovereigns, each enforcing its own law. This case, by contrast, arguably involves a single sovereign (the United States) that enforced its own law (the Major Crimes Act) after having separately enforced the law of another sovereign (the Code of the Ute Mountain Ute Tribe). Petitioner contends that the second prosecution violated the Double Jeopardy Clause because the dual-sovereignty doctrine requires that the offenses be both enacted *and* enforced by separate sovereigns.

We disagree. By its terms, the Clause prohibits separate prosecutions for the same offense; it does not bar successive prosecutions by the same sovereign. So even assuming that petitioner's first prosecutor exercised federal rather than tribal power, the second prosecution did not violate the Constitution's guarantee against double jeopardy.

I

In 1882, Secretary of the Interior H. M. Teller wrote to his Department's Office of Indian Affairs (now known as the Bureau of Indian Affairs) to suggest that the Office "formulate certain rules for the government of the Indians on the reservations." Letter to H. Price, Comm'r of Indian Affairs (Dec. 2, 1882), in Dept. of Interior, Rules Governing the Court of Indian Offenses 3-4 (1883). In response, the Commissioner of Indian Affairs adopted regulations prohibiting certain acts and directing that a "Court of Indian Offenses" be established for nearly every Indian tribe or group of tribes to adjudicate rule violations. Given their basis in what is now the Code of Federal Regulations, the courts are sometimes called CFR courts.

Today, most tribes have established their own judicial systems, thereby displacing the CFR courts. But some tribes, often due to resource constraints, have not. Five CFR courts remain, serving 16 of the more than 500 federally recognized tribes. Their stated purpose is "to provide adequate machinery for the administration of justice for Indian tribes" in certain parts of Indian country "where tribal courts have not been established." The Department's Assistant Secretary for Indian Affairs appoints CFR court judges, called magistrates, subject to a confirmation vote by the governing body of the tribe that the court serves. The Assistant Secretary may remove magistrates for cause of his own accord or upon the recommendation of the tribal governing body.[1] Unless a contract with a tribe provides otherwise, a Department official appoints the prosecutor for each CFR court.

CFR courts have jurisdiction over two sets of crimes. First, federal regulations set forth a list of offenses that may be enforced in CFR court. In addition, a tribe's governing body may enact ordinances that, when approved by the Assistant Secretary, are enforceable in CFR court and supersede any conflicting federal regulations.

The reservation of the Ute Mountain Ute Tribe spans over 500,000 acres in southwestern Colorado, northern New Mexico, and southeastern Utah. The Tribe has more than 2,000 members. It has not created its own court system, so it makes use of the Southwest Region CFR Court. The Tribe has, however, adopted its own penal code, which is enforceable in that court.

A violation of the tribal code lies at the heart of this case. Merle Denezpi and V. Y., both members of the Navajo Nation, traveled to Towaoc, Colorado, a town within the Ute Mountain Ute Reservation. While the two were alone at a house belonging to Denezpi's friend, Denezpi barricaded the door, threatened V. Y.,

---

[1] The CFR court at issue in this case serves only the Ute Mountain Ute Tribe. Some CFR courts, however, serve multiple tribes. In that event, the governing bodies of all affected tribes participate in the confirmation and removal of magistrates.

and forced her to have sex with him. After Denezpi fell asleep, V. Y. escaped from the house and reported Denezpi to tribal authorities.

An officer with the federal Bureau of Indian Affairs filed a criminal complaint in CFR court. That complaint charged Denezpi with three crimes: assault and battery, in violation of 6 Ute Mountain Ute Code §2 (1988); terroristic threats, in violation of 25 CFR §11.402; and false imprisonment, in violation of 25 CFR §11.404. Denezpi pleaded guilty to the assault and battery charge, and the prosecutor dismissed the other charges. The Magistrate sentenced Denezpi to time served — 140 days' imprisonment.

Six months later, a federal grand jury in the District of Colorado indicted Denezpi on one count of aggravated sexual abuse in Indian country, an offense covered by the federal Major Crimes Act. 18 U. S. C. §§2241(a)(1), (a)(2), 1153(a). Denezpi moved to dismiss the indictment, arguing that the Double Jeopardy Clause barred the consecutive prosecution, but the District Court denied the motion. After a jury convicted Denezpi, the District Court sentenced him to 360 months' imprisonment.

The Tenth Circuit affirmed. It concluded that the second prosecution in federal court did not constitute double jeopardy because the Ute Mountain Ute Tribe's inherent sovereignty was the ultimate source of power undergirding the earlier prosecution in CFR court.

II

The Double Jeopardy Clause of the Fifth Amendment provides: "No person shall . . . be subject for the same offence to be twice put in jeopardy of life or limb." The Clause by its terms does not prohibit twice placing a person in jeopardy "'for the same *conduct* or *actions*.'" *Gamble v. United States* (2019). Instead, it focuses on whether successive prosecutions are for the same "offence."

That term, we have explained, "'was commonly understood in 1791 to mean "transgression," that is, "the Violation or Breaking of a Law."'" An offense, then, is "defined by a law." And a law is defined by the sovereign that makes it, expressing the interests that the sovereign wishes to vindicate. Because the sovereign source of a law is an inherent and distinctive feature of the law itself, an offense defined by one sovereign is necessarily a different offense from that of another sovereign. That means that the two offenses can be separately prosecuted without offending the Double Jeopardy Clause — even if they have identical elements and could not be separately prosecuted if enacted by a single sovereign. See *Gamble*.

This dual-sovereignty principle applies where "two entities derive their power to punish from wholly independent sources." The doctrine has come up most frequently in the context of the States. See, *e.g., Heath v. Alabama* (1985) (States are separate sovereigns from one another); *Lanza* (1922) (States are separate sovereigns from the United States). It applies, however, to Indian tribes too.

United States v. Wheeler (1978), is the seminal case. There, a member of the Navajo Tribe was convicted in tribal court of violating a provision of the Navajo Tribal Code; he was later charged in federal court with violating a federal statute based on the same underlying conduct. Citing the dual-sovereignty doctrine, the Court rejected Wheeler's double jeopardy argument. We explained that before Europeans arrived on this continent, tribes "were self-governing sovereign political communities" with "the inherent power to prescribe laws for their members and to punish infractions of those laws." While "Congress has in certain ways regulated the manner and extent of the tribal power of self government," Congress did not "*creat[e]* " that power. When a tribe enacts criminal laws, then, "it does so as part of its retained sovereignty and not as an arm of the Federal Government." Thus, Wheeler's prosecution for a tribal offense did not bar his later prosecution for a federal offense.

Our reasoning in *Wheeler* controls here. Denezpi's single act transgressed two laws: the Ute Mountain Ute Code's assault and battery ordinance and the United States Code's proscription of aggravated sexual abuse in Indian country. The Ute Mountain Ute Tribe, like the Navajo Tribe in *Wheeler*, exercised its "unique" sovereign authority in adopting the tribal ordinance. Likewise, Congress exercised the United States' sovereign power in enacting the federal criminal statute. The two laws, defined by separate sovereigns, therefore proscribe separate offenses. Because Denezpi's second prosecution did not place him in jeopardy again "for the same offence," that prosecution did not violate the Double Jeopardy Clause.

Denezpi agrees with much of this — that sovereigns define distinct offenses, that the Tribe and the United States are separate sovereigns, and that his prosecutions involved a tribal offense and a federal offense respectively. But he argues that the dual-sovereignty doctrine is concerned not only with who defines the offense, but also with who *prosecutes* it. In *Wheeler*, the defendant was initially prosecuted in a tribal court; Denezpi, by contrast, was initially prosecuted in a CFR court. While tribal prosecutors in tribal courts indisputably exercise tribal authority, Denezpi claims that prosecutors in CFR courts exercise federal authority because they are subject to the control of the Bureau of Indian Affairs. He concludes that he was therefore prosecuted twice by the United States. And that, he insists, violated the Double Jeopardy Clause because "the dual-sovereignty doctrine does not apply when successive prosecutions are undertaken by a single sovereign, regardless of the source of the power to adopt the criminal codes enforced in each prosecution."

We need not sort out whether prosecutors in CFR courts exercise tribal or federal authority because we disagree with Denezpi's premise. The Double Jeopardy Clause does *not* prohibit successive prosecutions by the same sovereign. It prohibits successive prosecutions "for the same offence." And as we have already explained, an offense defined by one sovereign is different from an offense defined by another. Thus, even if Denezpi is right that the Federal Government prosecuted his tribal offense, the Clause did not bar the Federal Government from prosecuting him under the Major Crimes Act too.

Denezpi does not even try to reconcile his position with the text of the Clause. Instead, he presents the dual-sovereignty doctrine as "a carveout to the rule against double jeopardy" and argues that the carveout does not extend to successive prosecutions by a single sovereign. But Denezpi is wrong to treat the dual-sovereignty doctrine as an exception to the Clause. *Gamble* was very clear on this point: "Although the dual-sovereignty rule is often dubbed an 'exception' to the double jeopardy right, it is not an exception at all. On the contrary, it follows from the text that defines that right in the first place." The Clause does not ask who puts a person in jeopardy. It zeroes in on what the person is put in jeopardy for: the "offence." And again, in 1791, "offence" meant the violation of a law. We have seen no evidence that "offence" was originally understood to encompass both the violation of the law and the identity of the prosecutor.

Treating the identity of the prosecutor as part of the definition of "offence" is as odd as it sounds. An offense has always referred to the crime itself, which is complete when a person has carried out all of its elements. The law has long recognized, then, that an offense is committed before it is prosecuted. So Denezpi's proposal would put us in the position of holding that a person's single act constitutes two separate offenses at the time of commission (because the act violates two different sovereigns' laws) but that those offenses later become the same offense if a single sovereign prosecutes both. He offers no textual justification for this nonsensical result.

With the text against him, the best Denezpi can do is stitch together loose language from our precedent. For example, we have said that "two offenses 'are not the "same offence" ' for double jeopardy purposes if 'prosecuted by different sovereigns.'" *Gamble*. In another case, we stated that "[i]f an entity's authority to enact and enforce criminal law ultimately comes from Congress, then it cannot follow a federal prosecution with its own." And we have remarked that "the crucial determination [under the dual-sovereignty doctrine] is whether the two entities that seek successively to prosecute a defendant for the same course of conduct can be termed separate sovereigns."

Read in isolation, these statements help Denezpi's position that the identity of the prosecuting sovereign matters under the dual-sovereignty doctrine. Read in context, their helpfulness dissipates. None of these cases involves or even mentions the unusual situation of a single sovereign successively prosecuting its own law and that of a different sovereign. This language appears in the context of the usual situation: a sovereign (or alleged sovereign) prosecuting its own laws. Because enactment and enforcement almost always go hand in hand, it is easy to overlook that they are occasionally separated. That is particularly good reason to take the language Denezpi offers with a healthy sprinkling of salt. Where it was not important to attend to the difference between enactment and enforcement, it is understandable why we did not. In any event, imprecise statements cannot overcome the holdings of our cases, not to mention the text of the Clause—and those authorities make clear that enactment is what counts in determining whether the dual-sovereignty doctrine applies.

Denezpi points to only one case in which the Court dealt with an argument in the neighborhood of his. In *Bartkus v. Illinois* (1959), the defendant argued that his acquittal in federal court for a federal offense barred his later conviction in state court for a state offense based on the same underlying conduct. There was a threshold issue of whether to analyze the claim under the Fifth Amendment's Double Jeopardy Clause or the Fourteenth Amendment's Due Process Clause. The Double Jeopardy Clause had not yet been incorporated against the States, but the defendant argued that federal authorities had run his state prosecution, making it federal action to which the Clause applied. The Court rejected that argument, seeing no basis to say that "Illinois in bringing its prosecution was merely a tool of the federal authorities," rendering the "state prosecution . . . a sham and a cover for a federal prosecution." That resolution meant that the Court had no occasion to consider whether the Double Jeopardy Clause would have barred the Federal Government from separately prosecuting Bartkus for a violation of state law. Instead, we considered whether Bartkus' successive federal and state prosecutions violated due process.

Bartkus does not give Denezpi much to go on—as Denezpi himself recognizes. At most, *Bartkus* acknowledged that a successive federal prosecution would raise a double jeopardy question. Yet it did not begin to analyze, much less answer, that question. In the end, then, *Bartkus* is no more help to Denezpi than the other cases on which he relies.

Denezpi advances a few other arguments for why the Double Jeopardy Clause barred his second prosecution. None succeeds.

First, he notes that the United States has excluded from the string of federal regulatory offenses enforceable in CFR court those "[f]elonies that are covered by the Major Crimes Act." And it has done so "to avoid the possibility that someone who has committed a serious offense may be immunized from federal prosecution [under that Act] because of the prohibition against double jeopardy by a prosecution in a Court of Indian Offenses." Denezpi asserts that this "limitation borders on a concession that the Double Jeopardy Clause bars [his] second prosecution." We disagree. Federal regulatory crimes are defined by the Federal Government, so successive prosecutions for a federal regulatory crime and a federal statutory crime present a different double jeopardy question from the one presented here.

Next, Denezpi argues that permitting successive prosecutions like his "does not further the purposes underlying the dual-sovereignty doctrine," namely, advancing sovereigns' independent interests. [T]he Tribe's sovereign interest *is* furthered when its assault and battery ordinance—duly enacted by its governing body as an expression of the Tribe's condemnation of that crime—is enforced, regardless of who enforces it.

Finally, Denezpi asserts that the conclusion we reach might lead to "highly troubling" results. He suggests that sovereigns might more broadly assume the authority to enforce other sovereigns' criminal laws in order to get two bites at the apple. But if there is a constitutional barrier to such cross-enforcement, it does not derive from the Double Jeopardy Clause. As we have explained, the Clause does not bar successive prosecutions of distinct offenses, even if a single sovereign prosecutes them.

Denezpi's single act led to separate prosecutions for violations of a tribal ordinance and a federal statute. Because the Tribe and the Federal Government are distinct sovereigns, those "offence[s]" are not "the same." Denezpi's second prosecution therefore did not offend the Double Jeopardy Clause.

Justice GORSUCH, with whom Justice SOTOMAYOR and Justice KAGAN join as to Parts I and III, dissenting.

Federal prosecutors tried Merle Denezpi twice for the same crime. First, they charged him with violating a federal regulation. Then, they charged him with violating an overlapping federal statute. Same defendant, same crime, same prosecuting authority. Yet according to the Court, the Double Jeopardy Clause has nothing to say about this case. How can that be? To justify its conclusion, the Court invokes the dual-sovereignty doctrine. For reasons I have offered previously, I believe that doctrine is at odds with the text and original meaning of the Constitution. But even taking it at face value, the doctrine cannot sustain the Court's conclusion.

I

To appreciate why, some background about the Court of Indian Offenses helps. Unlike a tribal court operated by a Native American Tribe pursuant to its inherent sovereign authority, the Court of Indian Offenses is "part of the Federal Government." Really, it is a creature of the Department of the Interior. Secretary H. M. Teller opened the court by administrative decree in 1883. As he put it, the court was designed to "civilize the Indians" by forcing them to "desist from the savage and barbarous practices . . . calculated to continue them in savagery." Apparently, the Secretary and his contemporaries worried that too many Tribes were under "the influence of medicine men" and "without law of any kind," and they thought the Interior Department needed to take a strong hand to impose "some rule of government on the reservations."

Toward these ends, the Secretary instructed the Commissioner of Indian Affairs to promulgate "certain rules" to establish a new "tribunal" and to define new "offenses of which it was to take cognizance." The resulting "court" was composed of magistrates appointed by the Department who could "read and write English readily, w[ore] citizens' dress, and engage[d] in civilized pursuits." The Department likewise appointed officers charged with investigating the crimes it created. Federal Office of Child Support Enforcement. And the regulatory criminal code the Department produced outlawed everything from "old heathenish dances" and "medicine men" and their "conjurers' arts" to certain Indian mourning practices. The Department's new criminal code also assimilated "the laws of the State or Territory within which the reservation may be located," and instructed that sentences for assimilated offenses should match those imposed by state or territorial law. Unsurprisingly, tribal members often regarded these courts as "foreign" and "hated" institutions.

Over time, as the federal government's attitude toward Native American traditions changed, the Department adjusted certain aspects of its regime. Now, some of the old federal offenses aimed at punishing tribal customs are gone. But the regulations still list many crimes created by federal agency officials. 25 CFR §§11.400-11.454 (2021). And the regulations continue to assimilate other crimes too. Instead of assimilating state and territorial crimes, federal regulations today assimilate tribal crimes. They do so, however, only if and to the extent those tribal crimes are "approved by the Assistant Secretary [of] Indian Affairs or his or her designee."

These arrangements turned out to play a pivotal role in Mr. Denezpi's case. In July 2017, he traveled to visit his girlfriend in Towaoc, Colorado, a town within the Ute Mountain Ute Reservation. His traveling companion, a woman known as V. Y., alleged that during the visit Mr. Denezpi sexually assaulted her. Mr. Denezpi claimed the encounter was consensual. Both Mr. Denezpi and V. Y. are members of the Navajo Nation.

After a brief investigation, an agent of the Department of the Interior swore out a criminal complaint on behalf of the "United States of America. Federal officials charged Mr. Denezpi with three offenses: terroristic threats, false imprisonment, and assault and battery. Federal regulations define the first two offenses. See 25 CFR §§11.402, 11.404. The third offense—assault and battery—is an assimilated Ute Mountain Ute tribal offense "approved" by federal officials. §11.449. Ultimately, federal authorities dismissed the first two charges and Mr. Denezpi pleaded no contest to the third while maintaining his innocence. Pursuant to federal regulation, the court was empowered to sentence Mr. Denezpi to no more than six months in prison for his crime, the maximum punishment the assimilated tribal law permits. Ultimately, the court sentenced him to 140 days—a punishment just shy of the maximum.

After further consideration, it seems federal authorities may have regretted their hasty prosecution. It seems too they may have considered the punishment authorized by tribal law and their own regulations insufficient. Six months after Mr. Denezpi finished his Interior Department sentence, the Justice Department brought new charges against him for the same offense under federal statutory law. These new charges carried the potential for a much longer sentence, one unconnected to tribal judgments about the appropriate punishments for tribal members. See 18 U. S. C. §§2241(a), 1153(a). In time, a federal district court convicted Mr. Denezpi and sentenced him to an additional 30 years in prison, followed by 10 years of supervised release.

14.   Double Jeopardy

Throughout, Mr. Denezpi has argued that the Constitution's Double Jeopardy Clause barred his second prosecution. The Clause provides that no person shall be "twice put in jeopardy" "for the same offense." No one disputes that Mr. Denezpi's first crime of conviction (assault and battery) is a lesser included offense of his second crime of conviction (aggravated sexual abuse). And no one disputes that, under our precedents, that is normally enough to render them the "same offense" and forbid a second prosecution. *Blockburger v. United States* (1932). Yet both the District Court and Court of Appeals rejected Mr. Denezpi's argument, so he brought it here.

II

This Court has long recognized that, unless carefully cabined, the dual-sovereignty doctrine can present serious dangers. Taken to its extreme, it might allow prosecutors to coordinate and treat an initial trial in one jurisdiction as a dress rehearsal for a second trial in another. All of which would amount, in substance if not form, to successive trials for the same offense. For reasons like these, this Court has said repeatedly that the doctrine applies only when two requirements are satisfied. First, the two prosecutions must be brought under "the laws of two sovereigns." Second, the "two prosecuting *entities*" must "derive their power to punish from wholly independent [sovereign] sources." Here, neither condition is satisfied.

Start with the fact that both of Mr. Denezpi's convictions were for federal offenses. Almost in passing and with little analysis, the Court suggests that his first conviction was for a tribal offense and only his second involved a federal offense. But that is wrong. Mr. Denezpi's first prosecution in the Court of Indian Offenses was for the violation of federal regulations that assimilated tribal law into federal law.

The regulations could not be plainer. Subpart D of the regulations governing the Court of Indian Offenses is titled "Criminal Offenses." 25 CFR §§11.400-11.454. This subpart contains a list of federal regulatory crimes, many of which contain enumerated elements. Nested in this list is "§11.449: Violation of an approved tribal ordinance." That regulation declares that anyone who violates a tribal ordinance "approved by the Assistant Secretary [of] Indian Affairs" is "guilty of an offense"—that is, an offense under the Interior Department's own "Law and Order Code."

That is exactly what happened in Mr. Denezpi's first prosecution. The Ute Mountain Ute have a tribal offense of assault and battery. By all indications, it was "approved" by the Assistant Secretary for assimilation into federal regulations. And for this federal regulatory crime, Mr. Denezpi was sentenced to a term of incarceration in a federal detention center. On any reasonable account, Mr. Denezpi was not convicted of a tribal offense. He was convicted of violating §11.449, which assimilates federally approved tribal ordinances into federal law.

Both text and context indicate that Mr. Denezpi was prosecuted in the Court of Indian Offenses for a federal crime, not a tribal one. That is the best reading of the relevant regulations.

III

To honor the Double Jeopardy Clause in substance as well as form, our cases indicate that we must ask, among other things, whether "the 'entities that seek successively to prosecute a defendant . . . [are] separate sovereigns,'" based on "the deepest wellsprings . . . of [their] prosecutorial authority." "Whether two prosecuting entities are dual sovereigns in the double jeopardy context, we have stated, depends on whether they draw their authority to punish the offender from distinct sources of power. The inquiry is thus historical." Under this inquiry, "[i]f two entities derive their power to punish from wholly independent sources . . . then they may bring successive prosecutions. Conversely, if those entities draw their power from the same ultimate source . . . then they may not."

Applying these principles here, it is clear that the deepest historical well-springs of the Court of Indian Offenses' authority lie not in the Ute Mountain Ute or any other Tribe, but in the halls of the Department of the Interior. As we have seen, federal administrative authorities created this tribunal. Even today, federal officials continue to define and approve offenses for enforcement before it. They amend their list of offenses from time to time. They control the hiring and firing of prosecutors and magistrates. They opened this court; they may close it. The Court of Indian Offenses was and remains a federal scheme.

It would be deeply revisionist to suggest otherwise. The facts of this case drive the point home. Federal authorities brought charges against Mr. Denezpi in his first prosecution in the name of the United States. Those who prosecuted him were employed and controlled by the federal government. He was sentenced by a magistrate whom the federal government had the right to appoint and remove. And for his crime, Mr. Denezpi was incarcerated in a federal detention center. Federal agency officials played every meaningful role in his case: legislator, prosecutor, judge, and jailor.

There is more too. Federal authorities apparently regretted their hasty first prosecution. And far from seeking to vindicate tribal sentencing policy, it seems they may have found it wanting. So six months after the Interior Department finished the first case, the Justice Department took up the second.

[T]he dual-sovereignty doctrine has never exalted form over substance in this way. If taken to its extreme, the Court's reasoning could seemingly allow a State to punish an individual twice for identical offenses, so long as one is proscribed by state law and the other by federal law. It would potentially allow the federal government to do the same. This Court has never before endorsed such a parsimonious and easily evaded understanding of the Double Jeopardy Clause.

It is hard to believe this Court would long tolerate a similar state of affairs in any other context—allowing federal bureaucrats to define an offense; prosecute, judge, and punish an individual for it; and then transfer the case to the resident U. S. Attorney for a second trial for the same offense under federal statutory law. Still, for over a century that regime has persisted in this country for Native Americans, and today the Court extends its seal of approval to at least one aspect of it. Worse, the Court does so in the name of vindicating tribal sovereign authority. The irony will not be lost on those whose rights are diminished by today's decision. Respectfully, I dissent.

Chapter 15

HABEAS CORPUS

B. The Issues that Must Be Addressed in Order for a Federal Court to Grant Habeas Corpus Relief

4. Does the Petition Rely on Existing Rules or Seek Recognition of a New Rule of Constitutional Law? (casebook p. 1230)

In *Teague v. Lane*, the Supreme Court held that a federal court may adjudicate a habeas corpus petition asserting a "new rule" of constitutional law only if it is one that would apply retroactively. The Court has elaborated two exceptions where a rule of criminal procedure would apply retroactively: if it is a substantive change in the law or if it is a "watershed rule" of criminal procedure. Since *Teague* in 1989, the Court never found anything to constitute a new watershed rule of criminal procedure. In *Edwards v. Vannoy* (2021), the Supreme Court expressly overruled that aspect of *Teague* and held that no longer is there retroactivity based on there being a watershed rule of criminal procedure.

The year before, in *Ramos v. Louisiana* (2020), the Court held that the Sixth Amendment's requirement for a unanimous jury verdict is incorporated and applies to state governments. (This is presented in Chapter 1). The issue in *Edwards* was whether this applies retroactively to those who were convicted by non-unanimous juries before *Ramos*. The Court held that *Ramos* does not apply retroactively.

Edwards v. Vannoy
141 S. Ct. 1547 (2021)

Justice KAVANAUGH delivered the opinion of the Court.

Last Term in *Ramos v. Louisiana* (2020), this Court held that a state jury must be unanimous to convict a criminal defendant of a serious offense. *Ramos* repudiated this Court's 1972 decision in which had allowed non-unanimous juries in state criminal trials. The question in this case is whether the new rule of criminal procedure announced in *Ramos* applies retroactively to overturn final convictions on federal collateral review. Under this Court's retroactivity precedents, the answer is no.

This Court has repeatedly stated that a decision announcing a new rule of criminal procedure ordinarily does not apply retroactively on federal collateral review. See *Teague v. Lane*, (1989) Indeed, in the 32 years since *Teague* under-scored that principle, this Court has announced many important new rules of criminal procedure. But the Court has not applied *any* of those new rules retroactively on federal collateral review. And for decades before *Teague*, the Court also regularly declined to apply new rules retroactively, including on federal collateral review.

In light of the Court's well-settled retroactivity doctrine, we conclude that the *Ramos* jury-unanimity rule likewise does not apply retroactively on federal collateral review.

A new rule of criminal procedure applies to cases on *direct* review, even if the defendant's trial has already concluded. But under the habeas corpus statute as interpreted by this Court, a new rule of criminal procedure ordinarily does not apply retroactively to overturn final convictions on federal *collateral* review.

In stating that new procedural rules ordinarily do not apply retroactively on federal collateral review, *Teague* reinforced what had already been the Court's regular practice for several decades under the retroactivity standard articulated in *Linkletter v. Walker* (1965).

Put simply, the "costs imposed upon the States by retroactive application of new rules of constitutional law on habeas corpus thus generally far outweigh the benefits of this application." For that reason, the Court has repeatedly stated that new rules of criminal procedure ordinarily do not apply retroactively on federal collateral review.

The Court has identified only one possible exception to that principle. The Court has stated that a new procedural rule will apply retroactively on federal col-lateral review only if it constitutes a "watershed" rule of criminal procedure. But the *Teague* Court stated that it was "unlikely" that such watershed "components of basic due process have yet to emerge." And in the 32 years since *Teague*, as we will explain, the Court has *never* found that any new procedural rule actually satisfies that purported exception.

To determine whether *Ramos* applies retroactively on federal collateral review, we must answer two questions. First, did *Ramos* announce a new rule of criminal procedure, as opposed to applying a settled rule? A new rule ordi-narily does not apply retroactively on federal collateral review. Second, if *Ramos* announced a new rule, does it fall within an exception for watershed rules of criminal procedure that apply retroactively on federal collateral review?

Ramos held that a state jury must be unanimous to convict a defendant of a serious offense. In so holding, *Ramos* announced a new rule. A rule is new unless it was "*dictated* by precedent existing at the time the defendant's convic-tion became final." In other words, a rule is new unless, at the time the convic-tion became final, the rule was already "apparent to all reasonable jurists." The starkest example of a decision announcing a new rule is a decision that overrules an earlier case.

The jury-unanimity requirement announced in *Ramos* was not dictated by precedent or apparent to all reasonable jurists when Edwards's conviction became final in 2011. By renouncing *Apodaca* and expressly requiring unanimous jury verdicts in state criminal trials, *Ramos* plainly announced a new rule for purposes of this Court's retroactivity doctrine. And new rules of criminal procedure ordinarily do not apply retroactively on federal collateral review.

Having determined that *Ramos* announced a new rule requiring jury unanimity, we must consider whether that new rule falls within an exception for watershed rules of criminal procedure that apply retroactively on federal collateral review. This Court has stated that the watershed exception is "extremely narrow" and applies only when, among other things, the new rule alters "our understanding of the bedrock procedural elements essential to the fairness of a proceeding."

In the abstract, those various adjectives—watershed, narrow, bedrock, essential—do not tell us much about whether a particular decision of this Court qualifies for the watershed exception. In practice, the exception has been theoretical, not real. The Court has identified only one pre-*Teague* procedural rule as watershed: the right to counsel recognized in the Court's landmark decision in *Gideon v. Wainwright* (1963). The Court has never identified any other pre-*Teague* or post-*Teague* rule as watershed. None.

Moreover, the Court has flatly proclaimed on multiple occasions that the watershed exception is unlikely to cover any more new rules. Even 32 years ago in *Teague* itself, the Court stated that it was "unlikely" that additional watershed rules would "emerge." And since *Teague*, the Court has often reiterated that "it is unlikely that any such rules have yet to emerge."

Consistent with those many emphatic pronouncements, the Court since *Teague* has rejected *every* claim that a new procedural rule qualifies as a watershed rule.

If landmark and historic criminal procedure decisions do not apply retroactively on federal collateral review, how can any additional new rules of criminal procedure apply retroactively on federal collateral review? At this point, some 32 years after *Teague*, we think the only candid answer is that none can—that is, no new rules of criminal procedure can satisfy the watershed exception. We cannot responsibly continue to suggest otherwise to litigants and courts.

Continuing to articulate a theoretical exception that never actually applies in practice offers false hope to defendants, distorts the law, misleads judges, and wastes the resources of defense counsel, prosecutors, and courts. Moreover, no one can reasonably rely on an exception that is non-existent in practice, so no reliance interests can be affected by forthrightly acknowledging reality. It is time—probably long past time—to make explicit what has become increasingly apparent to bench and bar over the last 32 years: New procedural rules do not apply retroactively on federal collateral review. The watershed exception is moribund. It must "be regarded as retaining no vitality."

To summarize the Court's retroactivity principles: New substantive rules alter "the range of conduct or the class of persons that the law punishes." Those new substantive rules apply to cases pending in trial courts and on direct review, and they also apply retroactively on federal collateral review. New procedural rules alter "only the manner of determining the defendant's culpability." Those new procedural rules apply to cases pending in trial courts and on direct review. But new procedural rules do not apply retroactively on federal collateral review.

Ramos announced a new rule of criminal procedure. It does not apply retroactively on federal collateral review.

Justice KAGAN, with whom Justice BREYER and Justice SOTOMAYOR join, dissenting.

"A verdict, taken from eleven, [i]s no verdict at all," this Court proclaimed just last Term. (2020) Citing centuries of history, the Court in *Ramos* termed the Sixth Amendment right to a unanimous jury "vital," "essential," "indispensable," and "fundamental" to the American legal system. The Court therefore saw fit to disregard *stare decisis* and overturn a 50-year-old precedent enabling States to convict criminal defendants based on non-unanimous verdicts. And in taking that weighty step, the Court also vindicated core principles of racial justice. For in the Court's view, the state laws countenancing non-unanimous verdicts originated in white supremacism and continued in our own time to have racially discriminatory effects. Put all that together, and it is easy to see why the opinions in *Ramos* read as historic. Rarely does this Court make such a fundamental change in the rules thought necessary to ensure fair criminal process. If you were scanning a thesaurus for a single word to describe the decision, you would stop when you came to "watershed."

Yet the Court insists that *Ramos*'s holding does not count as a "watershed" procedural rule under The result of today's ruling is easily stated. *Ramos* will not apply retroactively, meaning that a prisoner whose appeals ran out before the decision can receive no aid from the change in law it made. So Thedrick Edwards, unlike Evangelisto Ramos, will serve the rest of his life in prison based on a 10-to-2 jury verdict. Only the reasoning of today's holding resists explanation. The majority cannot (and indeed does not) deny, given all *Ramos* said, that the jury unanimity requirement fits to a tee *Teague*'s description of a watershed procedural rule. Nor can the majority explain its result by relying on precedent. Although flaunting decisions since *Teague* that held rules non-retroactive, the majority comes up with none comparable to this case. Search high and low the settled law of retroactivity, and the majority still has no reason to deny *Ramos* watershed status.

So everything rests on the majority's last move—the overturning of *Teague*'s watershed exception. If there can never be *any* watershed rules—as the majority here asserts out of the blue—then, yes, jury unanimity cannot be one. The result follows trippingly from the premise. But adopting the premise requires departing from judicial practice and principle. In overruling a critical aspect of *Teague*, the majority follows none of the usual rules of *stare decisis*. It discards precedent without a party requesting that action. And it does so with barely a reason given, much less the "special justification" our law demands. The majority in that way compounds its initial error: Not content to misapply *Teague*'s watershed provision here, the majority forecloses any future application. It prevents any procedural rule ever—no matter how integral to adjudicative fairness—from benefiting a defendant on habeas review. Thus does a settled principle of retroactivity law die, in an effort to support an insupportable ruling.

And putting talk of *stare decisis* aside, there remains much more in *Ramos* to echo *Teague*. If, as today's majority says, *Teague* is full of "adjectives," so too is *Ramos*—and mostly the same ones. Jury unanimity, the Court pronounced, is an "essential element[ ]" of the jury trial right, and thus is "fundamental to the American scheme of justice." The Court discussed the rule's "ancient" history—"400 years of English and American cases requiring unanimity" leading up to the Sixth Amendment. As early as the 14th century, English common law recognized jury unanimity as a "vital right." Adopting that view, the early American States likewise treated unanimity as an "essential feature of the jury trial." So by the time the Framers drafted the Sixth Amendment, "the right to a jury trial *meant* a trial in which the jury renders a unanimous verdict." Because that was so, no jury verdict could stand (or in some metaphysical sense, even exist) absent full agreement: "A verdict, taken from eleven, was no verdict at all." Unanimity served as a critical safeguard, needed to protect against wrongful deprivations of citizens' "hard-won liberty." Or as Justice Story summarized the law a few decades after the Founding: To obtain a conviction, "unanimity in the verdict of the jury is indispensable."

If a rule so understood isn't a watershed one, then nothing is. (And that is, of course, what the majority eventually says.) Once more, from the quotations just above: "fundamental," "essential," "vital," "indispensable." No wonder today's majority declares a new-found aversion to "adjectives"—or, as a concurring opinion says, "all these words." The unanimity rule, as *Ramos* described it, is as "bedrock" as bedrock comes. It is as grounded in the Nation's constitutional traditions—with centuries-old practice becoming part of the Sixth Amendment's original meaning. And it is as central to the Nation's idea of a fair and reliable guilty verdict.

So the majority is left to overrule *Teague*'s holding on watershed rules. On the last page or so of its merits discussion (before it turns to pre-butting this dissent), the majority eliminates the watershed exception, declaring it "long past time" to do so. *Teague* had said there would not be "many" (retroactive) watershed rules. The majority now says there will be none at all. If that is so, of course, jury unanimity cannot be watershed. Finally, the majority offers an intelligible reason for declining to apply *Ramos* retroactively.

But in taking that road, the majority breaks a core judicial rule: respect for precedent. *Stare decisis* is a foundation stone of the rule of law, "promot[ing] the evenhanded, predictable, and consistent development of legal principles, foster[ing] reliance on judicial decisions, and contribut[ing] to the actual and perceived integrity of the judicial process."

To begin with, no one here asked us to overrule *Teague*. This Court usually confines itself to the issues raised and briefed by the parties. There may be reasons to ignore that rule in one or another everyday case. But to do so in pursuit of over-turning precedent is nothing short of extraordinary.

Equally striking, the majority gives only the sketchiest of reasons for reversing *Teague*'s watershed exception. In deciding whether to depart from precedent, the Court usually considers—and usually at length—a familiar set of factors capable of providing the needed special justification. The majority can't be bothered with that customary, and disciplining, practice; it barely goes through the motions. Seldom has this Court so casually, so off-handedly, tossed aside precedent. In its page of analysis, the majority offers just one ground for its decision—that since *Teague*, the Court has not identified a new rule as watershed, and so "the purported exception has become an empty promise." But even viewed in the abstract, that argument does not fly. That the Court has not found a watershed rule since *Teague* does not mean it could or would not in the future. *Teague* itself understood that point: It saw value in the watershed exception even while recognizing that watershed rules would be few and far between. And viewed in the context of this case, the majority's argument positively craters. For the majority today comes face-to-face with a rule that perfectly fits each of *Teague*'s criteria: Jury unanimity, as described in *Ramos*, is watershed—even though no prior rule was. That airtight match between *Ramos* and *Teague* refutes the majority's one stated reason for overruling the latter decision. The majority could not rely on the absence of watershed rules to topple *Teague* if it had just faithfully applied that decision to this case.

I would not discard *Teague*'s watershed exception and so keep those unfairly convicted people from getting new trials. Instead, I would accept the consequences of last Term's holding in *Ramos*. A decision like that comes with a promise, or at any rate should. If the right to a unanimous jury is so fundamental—if a verdict rendered by a divided jury is "no verdict at all"—then Thedrick Edwards should not spend his life behind bars over two jurors' opposition. I respectfully dissent.

FEDERAL RULES OF CRIMINAL PROCEDURE

Rule 4.   Arrest Warrant or Summons on a Complaint

(a)   *Issuance.*

If the complaint or one or more affidavits filed with the complaint establish probable cause to believe that an offense has been committed and that the defendant committed it, the judge must issue an arrest warrant to an officer authorized to execute it. At the request of an attorney for the government, the judge must issue a summons, instead of a warrant, to a person authorized to serve it. A judge may issue more than one warrant or summons on the same complaint. If a defendant fails to appear in response to a summons, a judge may, and upon request of an attorney for the government must, issue a warrant. If an organizational defendant fails to appear in response to a summons, a judge may take any action authorized by United States law.

(b)   *Form.*

(1)   Warrant.

A warrant must:

(A) contain the defendant's name or, if it is unknown, a name or description by which the defendant can be identified with reasonable certainty;

(B) describe the offense charged in the complaint;

(C) command that the defendant be arrested and brought without unnecessary delay before a magistrate judge or, if none is reasonably available, before a state or local judicial officer; and

(D) be signed by a judge.

(2)   Summons.

A summons must be in the same form as a warrant except that it must require the defendant to appear before a magistrate judge at a stated time and place.

(c) *Execution or Service, and Return.*

   (1)   By Whom.

Only a marshal or other authorized officer may execute a warrant. Any person authorized to serve a summons in a federal civil action may serve a summons.

   (2)   Location.

A warrant may be executed, or a summons served, within the jurisdiction of the United States or anywhere else a federal statute authorizes an arrest. A summons to an organization under Rule 4(c)(3)(D) may also be served at a place not within a judicial district of the United States.

   (3)   Manner.

(A) A warrant is executed by arresting the defendant. Upon arrest, an officer possessing the original or a duplicate original warrant must show it to the defendant. If the officer does not possess the warrant, the officer must inform the defendant of the warrant's existence and of the offense charged and, at the defendant's request, must show the original or a duplicate original warrant to the defendant as soon as possible.

(B) A summons is served on an individual defendant:

   (i) by delivering a copy to the defendant personally; or

   (ii) by leaving a copy at the defendant's residence or usual place of abode with a person of suitable age and discretion residing at that location and by mailing a copy to the defendant's last known address.

   (C) A summons is served on an organization by delivering a copy to an officer, to a managing or general agent, or to another agent appointed or legally authorized to receive service of process. If the agent is one authorized by statute and the statute so requires, a copy must also be mailed to the organization.

* * *

   (4)   Return.

(A) After executing a warrant, the officer must return it to the judge before whom the defendant is brought in accordance with Rule 5. The officer may do so by reliable electronic means. At the request of an attorney for the government, an unexecuted warrant must be brought back to and canceled by a magistrate judge or, if none is reasonably available, by a state or local judicial officer.

(B) The person to whom a summons was delivered for service must return it on or before the return day.

(C) At the request of an attorney for the government, a judge may deliver an unexecuted warrant, an unserved summons, or a copy of the warrant or summons to the marshal or other authorized person for execution or service.

(d) Warrant by Telephone or Other Reliable Electronic Means.

In accordance with Rule 4.1, a magistrate judge may issue a warrant or summons based on information communicated by telephone or other reliable electronic means.

Rule 4.1.   Complaint, Warrant, or Summons by Telephone or Other Reliable Electronic Means

(a)   In General.

A magistrate judge may consider information communicated by telephone or other reliable electronic means when reviewing a complaint or deciding whether to issue a warrant or summons.

(b)   Procedures.

If a magistrate judge decides to proceed under this rule, the following procedures apply:

(1)   Taking Testimony Under Oath.

The judge must place under oath — and may examine — the applicant and any person on whose testimony the application is based.

(2)   Creating a Record of the Testimony and Exhibits.

(A) Testimony Limited to Attestation. If the applicant does no more than attest to the contents of a written affidavit submitted by reliable electronic means, the judge must acknowledge the attestation in writing on the affidavit.

(B) Additional Testimony or Exhibits. If the judge considers additional testimony or exhibits, the judge must:

(i) have the testimony recorded verbatim by an electronic recording device, by a court reporter, or in writing;

(ii) have any recording or reporter's notes transcribed, have the transcription certified as accurate, and file it;

(iii) sign any other written record, certify its accuracy, and file it; and

(iv) make sure that the exhibits are filed.

(3) Preparing a Proposed Duplicate Original of a Complaint, Warrant, or Summons.

The applicant must prepare a proposed duplicate original of a complaint, warrant, or summons, and must read or otherwise transmit its contents verbatim to the judge.

(4) Preparing an Original Complaint, Warrant, or Summons.

If the applicant reads the contents of the proposed duplicate original, the judge must enter those contents into an original complaint, warrant, or summons. If the applicant transmits the contents by reliable electronic means, the transmission received by the judge may serve as the original.

(5) Modification.

The judge may modify the complaint, warrant, or summons. The judge must then:

(A) transmit the modified version to the applicant by reliable electronic means; or

(B) file the modified original and direct the applicant to modify the proposed duplicate original accordingly.

(6) Issuance.

To issue the warrant or summons, the judge must:

(A) sign the original documents;

(B) enter the date and time of issuance on the warrant or summons; and

(C) transmit the warrant or summons by reliable electronic means to the applicant or direct the applicant to sign the judge's name and enter the date and time on the duplicate original.

(c) Suppression Limited.

Absent a finding of bad faith, evidence obtained from a warrant issued under this rule is not subject to suppression on the ground that issuing the warrant in this manner was unreasonable under the circumstances.

Rule 5.   Initial Appearance

(a) In General.

(1)   Appearance Upon an Arrest.

(A) A person making an arrest within the United States must take the defendant without unnecessary delay before a magistrate judge, or before a state or local judicial officer as Rule 5(c) provides, unless a statute provides otherwise.

(B) A person making an arrest outside the United States must take the defendant without unnecessary delay before a magistrate judge, unless a statute provides otherwise.

(2)   Exceptions.

(A) An officer making an arrest under a warrant issued upon a complaint charging solely a violation of 18 U.S.C. §1073 need not comply with this rule if:

(i) the person arrested is transferred without unnecessary delay to the custody of appropriate state or local authorities in the district of arrest; and

(ii) an attorney for the government moves promptly, in the district where the warrant was issued, to dismiss the complaint.

(B) If a defendant is arrested for violating probation or supervised release, Rule 32.1 applies.

(C) If a defendant is arrested for failing to appear in another district, Rule 40 applies.

(3)   Appearance Upon a Summons.

When a defendant appears in response to a summons under Rule 4, a magistrate judge must proceed under Rule 5(d) or (e), as applicable.

(b) Arrest Without a Warrant.

If a defendant is arrested without a warrant, a complaint meeting Rule 4(a)'s requirement of probable cause must be promptly filed in the district where the offense was allegedly committed.

(c) Place of Initial Appearance; Transfer to Another District.

(1) Arrest in the District Where the Offense Was Allegedly Committed.

If the defendant is arrested in the district where the offense was allegedly committed:

(A) the initial appearance must be in that district; and

(B) if a magistrate judge is not reasonably available, the initial appearance may be before a state or local judicial officer.

(2) Arrest in a District Other Than Where the Offense Was Allegedly Committed.

If the defendant was arrested in a district other than where the offense was allegedly committed, the initial appearance must be:

(A) in the district of arrest; or

(B) in an adjacent district if:

(i) the appearance can occur more promptly there; or

(ii) the offense was allegedly committed there and the initial appearance will occur on the day of arrest.

* * *

(d) Procedure in a Felony Case.

(1) Advice.

If the defendant is charged with a felony, the judge must inform the defendant of the following:

(A) the complaint against the defendant, and any affidavit filed with it;

(B) the defendant's right to retain counsel or to request that counsel be appointed if the defendant cannot obtain counsel;

(C) the circumstances, if any, under which the defendant may secure pretrial release;

(D) any right to a preliminary hearing; and

(E) the defendant's right not to make a statement, and that any statement made may be used against the defendant.

(F) that a defendant who is not a United States citizen may request that an attorney for the government or a federal law enforcement official notify a consular officer from the defendant's country of nationality that the defendant has been arrested – but that even without defendant's request, a treat or other international agreement may require consular notification.

    (2)   Consulting with Counsel.

The judge must allow the defendant reasonable opportunity to consult with counsel.

    (3)   Detention or Release.

The judge must detain or release the defendant as provided by statute or these rules.

    (4)   Plea.

A defendant may be asked to plead only under Rule 10.

(e)   *Procedure in a Misdemeanor Case.*

If the defendant is charged with a misdemeanor only, the judge must inform the defendant in accordance with Rule 58(b)(2).

(f)   *Reminder of Prosecutorial Obligation.*

    (1)   In General.

In all criminal proceedings, on the first scheduled court date when both prosecutor and defense counsel are present, the judge shall issue an oral and written order to prosecution and defense counsel that confirms the disclosure obligation of the prosecutor under Brady v. Maryland, 373 U.S. 83 (1963) and its progeny, and the possible consequences of violating such order under applicable law.

(2)   Formation of Order.

Each judicial council in which a district court is located shall promulgate a model order for the purpose of paragraph (1) that the court may use as it determines is appropriate.

(g) *Video Teleconferencing.*

Video teleconferencing may be used to conduct an appearance under this rule if the defendant consents.

Rule 5.1.   Preliminary Hearing

(a) *In General.*

If a defendant is charged with an offense other than a petty offense, a magistrate judge must conduct a preliminary hearing unless:

   (1)   the defendant waives the hearing;

   (2)   the defendant is indicted;

   (3)   the government files an information under Rule 7(b) charging the defendant with a felony;

   (4)   the government files an information charging the defendant with a misdemeanor; or

   (5)   the defendant is charged with a misdemeanor and consents to trial before a magistrate judge.

(b) *Selecting a District.*

A defendant arrested in a district other than where the offense was allegedly committed may elect to have the preliminary hearing conducted in the district where the prosecution is pending.

(c) *Scheduling.*

The magistrate judge must hold the preliminary hearing within a reasonable time, but no later than 14 days after the initial appearance if the defendant is in custody and no later than 21 days if not in custody.

(d)   Extending the Time.

With the defendant's consent and upon a showing of good cause—taking into account the public interest in the prompt disposition of criminal cases—a magistrate judge may extend the time limits in Rule 5.1(c) one or more times. If the defendant does not consent, the magistrate judge may extend the time limits only on a showing that extraordinary circumstances exist and justice requires the delay.

(e)   Hearing and Finding.

At the preliminary hearing, the defendant may cross-examine adverse witnesses and may introduce evidence but may not object to evidence on the ground that it was unlawfully acquired. If the magistrate judge finds probable cause to believe an offense has been committed and the defendant committed it, the magistrate judge must promptly require the defendant to appear for further proceedings.

(f)   Discharging the Defendant.

If the magistrate judge finds no probable cause to believe an offense has been committed or the defendant committed it, the magistrate judge must dismiss the complaint and discharge the defendant. A discharge does not preclude the government from later prosecuting the defendant for the same offense.

(g)   Recording the Proceedings.

The preliminary hearing must be recorded by a court reporter or by a suitable recording device. A recording of the proceeding may be made available to any party upon request. A copy of the recording and a transcript may be provided to any party upon request and upon any payment required by applicable Judicial Conference regulations.

(h)   Producing a Statement.

   (1)   In General.

Rule 26.2(a)-(d) and (f) applies at any hearing under this rule, unless the magistrate judge for good cause rules otherwise in a particular case.

   (2)   Sanctions for Not Producing a Statement.

If a party disobeys a Rule 26.2 order to deliver a statement to the moving party, the magistrate judge must not consider the testimony of a witness whose statement is withheld.

Rule 6.   The Grand Jury

(a)   *Summoning a Grand Jury.*

(1)   In General.

When the public interest so requires, the court must order that one or more grand juries be summoned. A grand jury must have 16 to 23 members, and the court must order that enough legally qualified persons be summoned to meet this requirement.

(2)   Alternate Jurors.

When a grand jury is selected, the court may also select alternate jurors. Alternate jurors must have the same qualifications and be selected in the same manner as any other juror. Alternate jurors replace jurors in the same sequence in which the alternates were selected. An alternate juror who replaces a juror is subject to the same challenges, takes the same oath, and has the same authority as the other jurors.

(b)   *Objection to the Grand Jury or to a Grand Juror.*

(1)   Challenges.

Either the government or a defendant may challenge the grand jury on the ground that it was not lawfully drawn, summoned, or selected, and may challenge an individual juror on the ground that the juror is not legally qualified.

(2)   Motion to Dismiss an Indictment.

A party may move to dismiss the indictment based on an objection to the grand jury or on an individual juror's lack of legal qualification, unless the court has previously ruled on the same objection under Rule 6(b)(1). The motion to dismiss is governed by 28 U.S.C. §1867(e). The court must not dismiss the indictment on the ground that a grand juror was not legally qualified if the record shows that at least 12 qualified jurors concurred in the indictment.

(c)   *Foreperson and Deputy Foreperson.*

The court will appoint one juror as the foreperson and another as the deputy foreperson. In the foreperson's absence, the deputy foreperson will act as the foreperson. The foreperson may administer oaths and affirmations and will sign all indictments. The foreperson—or another juror designated by the foreperson—will record the number of jurors concurring in every indictment and will file the record with the clerk, but the record may not be made public unless the court so orders.

(d) Who May Be Present.

(1) While the Grand Jury Is in Session.

The following persons may be present while the grand jury is in session: attorneys for the government, the witness being questioned, interpreters when needed, and a court reporter or an operator of a recording device.

(2) During Deliberations and Voting.

No person other than the jurors, and any interpreter needed to assist a hearing-impaired or speech-impaired juror, may be present while the grand jury is deliberating or voting.

(e) Recording and Disclosing the Proceedings.

(1) Recording the Proceedings.

Except while the grand jury is deliberating or voting, all proceedings must be recorded by a court reporter or by a suitable recording device. But the validity of a prosecution is not affected by the unintentional failure to make a recording. Unless the court orders otherwise, an attorney for the government will retain control of the recording, the reporter's notes, and any transcript prepared from those notes.

(2) Secrecy.

(A) No obligation of secrecy may be imposed on any person except in accordance with Rule 6(e)(2)(B).

(B) Unless these rules provide otherwise, the following persons must not disclose a matter occurring before the grand jury:

(i) a grand juror;

(ii) an interpreter;

(iii) a court reporter;

(iv) an operator of a recording device;

(v) a person who transcribes recorded testimony;

(vi) an attorney for the government; or

(vii) a person to whom disclosure is made under Rule 6(e)(3)(A)(ii) or (iii).

(3)   Exceptions.

(A) Disclosure of a grand-jury matter—other than the grand jury's deliberations or any grand juror's vote—may be made to:

(i) an attorney for the government for use in performing that attorney's duty;

(ii) any government personnel—including those of a state, state subdivision, Indian tribe, or foreign government—that an attorney for the government considers necessary to assist in performing that attorney's duty to enforce federal criminal law; or

(iii) a person authorized by 18 U.S.C. §3322.

(B) A person to whom information is disclosed under Rule 6(e)(3)(A)(ii) may use that information only to assist an attorney for the government in performing that attorney's duty to enforce federal criminal law. An attorney for the government must promptly provide the court that impaneled the grand jury with the names of all persons to whom a disclosure has been made, and must certify that the attorney has advised those persons of their obligation of secrecy under this rule.

(C) An attorney for the government may disclose any grand-jury matter to another federal grand jury.

(D) An attorney for the government may disclose any grand-jury matter involving foreign intelligence, counterintelligence (as defined in 50 U.S.C. §3003), or foreign intelligence information (as defined in Rule 6(e)(3)(D)(iii)) to any federal law enforcement, intelligence, protective, immigration, national defense, or national security official to assist the official receiving the information in the performance of that official's duties. An attorney for the government may also disclose any grand-jury matter involving, within the United States or elsewhere, a threat of attack or other grave hostile acts of a foreign power or its agent, a threat of domestic or international sabotage or terrorism, or clandestine intelligence gathering activities by an intelligence service or network of a foreign power or by its agent, to any appropriate federal, state, state subdivision, Indian tribal, or foreign government official, for the purpose of preventing or responding to such threat or activities.

(i) Any official who receives information under Rule 6(e)(3)(D) may use the information only as necessary in the conduct of that person's official duties subject to any limitations on the unauthorized disclosure of such information. Any state, state subdivision, Indian tribal, or foreign government official who receives information under Rule 6(e)(3)(D) may use the information only in a manner consistent with any guidelines issued by the Attorney General and the Director of National Intelligence.

(ii) Within a reasonable time after disclosure is made under Rule 6(e)(3)(D), an attorney for the government must file, under seal, a notice with the court in the district where the grand jury convened stating that such information was disclosed and the departments, agencies, or entities to which the disclosure was made.

(iii) As used in Rule 6(e)(3)(D), the term "foreign intelligence information" means:

(a) information, whether or not it concerns a United States person, that relates to the ability of the United States to protect against—

- actual or potential attack or other grave hostile acts of a foreign power or its agent;
- sabotage or international terrorism by a foreign power or its agent; or
- clandestine intelligence activities by an intelligence service or network of a foreign power or by its agent; or

(b) information, whether or not it concerns a United States person, with respect to a foreign power or foreign territory that relates to—

- the national defense or the security of the United States; or
- the conduct of the foreign affairs of the United States.

(E) The court may authorize disclosure—at a time, in a manner, and subject to any other conditions that it directs—of a grand-jury matter:

(i) preliminarily to or in connection with a judicial proceeding;

(ii) at the request of a defendant who shows that a ground may exist to dismiss the indictment because of a matter that occurred before the grand jury;

(iii) at the request of the government, when sought by a foreign court or prosecutor for use in an official criminal investigation;

(iv) at the request of the government if it shows that the matter may disclose a violation of State, Indian tribal, or foreign criminal law, as long as the disclosure is to an appropriate state, state-subdivision, Indian tribal, or foreign government official for the purpose of enforcing that law; or

(v) at the request of the government if it shows that the matter may disclose a violation of military criminal law under the Uniform Code of Military Justice, as long as the disclosure is to an appropriate military official for the purpose of enforcing that law.

(F) A petition to disclose a grand-jury matter under Rule 6(e)(3)(E)(i) must be filed in the district where the grand jury convened. Unless the hearing is ex parte—as it may be when the government is the petitioner—the petitioner must serve the petition on, and the court must afford a reasonable opportunity to appear and be heard to:

(i) an attorney for the government;

(ii) the parties to the judicial proceeding; and

(iii) any other person whom the court may designate.

(G) If the petition to disclose arises out of a judicial proceeding in another district, the petitioned court must transfer the petition to the other court unless the petitioned court can reasonably determine whether disclosure is proper. If the petitioned court decides to transfer, it must send to the transferee court the material sought to be disclosed, if feasible, and a written evaluation of the need for continued grand-jury secrecy. The transferee court must afford those persons identified in Rule 6(e)(3)(F) a reasonable opportunity to appear and be heard.

(4)   Sealed Indictment.

The magistrate judge to whom an indictment is returned may direct that the indictment be kept secret until the defendant is in custody or has been released pending trial. The clerk must then seal the indictment, and no person may disclose the indictment's existence except as necessary to issue or execute a warrant or summons.

(5)   Closed Hearing.

Subject to any right to an open hearing in a contempt proceeding, the court must close any hearing to the extent necessary to prevent disclosure of a matter occurring before a grand jury.

(6)   Sealed Records.

Records, orders, and subpoenas relating to grand-jury proceedings must be kept under seal to the extent and as long as necessary to prevent the unauthorized disclosure of a matter occurring before a grand jury.

(7)   Contempt.

A knowing violation of Rule 6, or of any guidelines jointly issued by the Attorney General and the Director of National Intelligence under Rule 6, may be punished as a contempt of court.

(f)   Indictment and Return.

A grand jury may indict only if at least 12 jurors concur. The grand jury—or its foreperson or deputy foreperson—must return the indictment to a magistrate judge in open court. To avoid unnecessary cost or delay, the magistrate may take the return by video conference from the court where the grand jury sits. If a complaint or information is pending against the defendant and 12 jurors do not concur in the indictment, the foreperson must promptly and in writing report the lack of concurrence to the magistrate judge.

(g)   Discharging the Grand Jury.

A grand jury must serve until the court discharges it, but it may serve more than 18 months only if the court, having determined that an extension is in the public interest, extends the grand jury's service. An extension may be granted for no more than 6 months, except as otherwise provided by statute.

(h)   Excusing a Juror.

At any time, for good cause, the court may excuse a juror either temporarily or permanently, and if permanently, the court may impanel an alternate juror in place of the excused juror.

(i) *"Indian Tribe" Defined.*

"Indian tribe" means an Indian tribe recognized by the Secretary of the Interior on a list published in the Federal Register under 25 U.S.C. §479a-1.

Rule 7. The Indictment and the Information

(a) *When Used.*

(1) Felony.

An offense (other than criminal contempt) must be prosecuted by an indictment if it is punishable:

(A) by death; or

(B) by imprisonment for more than one year.

(2) Misdemeanor.

An offense punishable by imprisonment for one year or less may be prosecuted in accordance with Rule 58(b)(1).

(b) *Waiving Indictment.*

An offense punishable by imprisonment for more than one year may be prosecuted by information if the defendant—in open court and after being advised of the nature of the charge and of the defendant's rights—waives prosecution by indictment.

(c) *Nature and Contents.*

(1) In General.

The indictment or information must be a plain, concise, and definite written statement of the essential facts constituting the offense charged and must be signed by an attorney for the government. It need not contain a formal introduction or conclusion. A count may incorporate by reference an allegation made in another count. A count may allege that the means by which the defendant committed the offense are unknown or that the defendant committed it by one or more specified means. For each count, the indictment or information must give the official or customary citation of the statute, rule, regulation, or other provision of law that the defendant is alleged to have violated. For purposes of an indictment referred to in section 3282 of title 18, United States Code, for which the identity of the defendant is unknown, it shall be sufficient for the indictment to describe the defendant as an individual whose name is unknown, but who has a particular DNA profile, as that term is defined in that section 3282.

(2)   Citation Error.

Unless the defendant was misled and thereby prejudiced, neither an error in a citation nor a citation's omission is a ground to dismiss the indictment or information or to reverse a conviction.

(d) Surplusage.

Upon the defendant's motion, the court may strike surplusage from the indictment or information.

(e) Amending an Information.

Unless an additional or different offense is charged or a substantial right of the defendant is prejudiced, the court may permit an information to be amended at any time before the verdict or finding.

(f)   Bill of Particulars.

The court may direct the government to file a bill of particulars. The defendant may move for a bill of particulars before or within 14 days after arraignment or at a later time if the court permits. The government may amend a bill of particulars subject to such conditions as justice requires.

Rule 8.   Joinder of Offenses or Defendants

(a)   Joinder of Offenses.

The indictment or information may charge a defendant in separate counts with 2 or more offenses if the offenses charged—whether felonies or misdemeanors or both—are of the same or similar character, or are based on the same act or transaction, or are connected with or constitute parts of a common scheme or plan.

(b)   Joinder of Defendants.

The indictment or information may charge 2 or more defendants if they are alleged to have participated in the same act or transaction, or in the same series of acts or transactions, constituting an offense or offenses. The defendants may be charged in one or more counts together or separately. All defendants need not be charged in each count.

Rule 11.   Pleas

(a)   Entering a Plea.

(1)   In General.

A defendant may plead not guilty, guilty, or (with the court's consent) nolo contendere.

(2)   Conditional Plea.

With the consent of the court and the government, a defendant may enter a conditional plea of guilty or nolo contendere, reserving in writing the right to have an appellate court review an adverse determination of a specified pretrial motion. A defendant who prevails on appeal may then withdraw the plea.

(3)   Nolo Contendere Plea.

Before accepting a plea of nolo contendere, the court must consider the parties' views and the public interest in the effective administration of justice.

(4)   Failure to Enter a Plea.

If a defendant refuses to enter a plea or if a defendant organization fails to appear, the court must enter a plea of not guilty.

(b)   Considering and Accepting a Guilty or Nolo Contendere Plea.

(1)   Advising and Questioning the Defendant.

Before the court accepts a plea of guilty or nolo contendere, the defendant may be placed under oath, and the court must address the defendant personally in open court. During this address, the court must inform the defendant of, and determine that the defendant understands, the following:

(A) the government's right, in a prosecution for perjury or false statement, to use against the defendant any statement that the defendant gives under oath;

(B) the right to plead not guilty, or having already so pleaded, to persist in that plea;

(C) the right to a jury trial;

(D) the right to be represented by counsel—and if necessary have the court appoint counsel—at trial and at every other stage of the proceeding;

(E) the right at trial to confront and cross-examine adverse witnesses, to be protected from compelled self-incrimination, to testify and present evidence, and to compel the attendance of witnesses;

(F) the defendant's waiver of these trial rights if the court accepts a plea of guilty or nolo contendere;

(G) the nature of each charge to which the defendant is pleading;

(H) any maximum possible penalty, including imprisonment, fine, and term of supervised release;

(I) any mandatory minimum penalty;

(J) any applicable forfeiture;

(K) the court's authority to order restitution;

(L) the court's obligation to impose a special assessment;

(M) in determining a sentence, the court's obligation to calculate the applicable sentencing-guideline range and to consider that range, possible departures under the Sentencing Guidelines, and other sentencing factors under 18 U.S.C. §3553(a);

(N) the terms of any plea-agreement provision waiving the right to appeal or to collaterally attack the sentence.

(O) that, if convicted, a defendant who is not a United States citizen may be removed from the United States, denied citizenship, and denied admission to the United States in the future.

(2)   Ensuring That a Plea Is Voluntary.

Before accepting a plea of guilty or nolo contendere, the court must address the defendant personally in open court and determine that the plea is voluntary and did not result from force, threats, or promises (other than promises in a plea agreement).

(3)   Determining the Factual Basis for a Plea.

Before entering judgment on a guilty plea, the court must determine that there is a factual basis for the plea.

(c)   *Plea Agreement Procedure.*

(1)   In General.

An attorney for the government and the defendant's attorney, or the defendant when proceeding pro se, may discuss and reach a plea agreement. The court must not participate in these discussions. If the defendant pleads guilty or nolo contendere to either a charged offense or a lesser or related offense, the plea agreement may specify that an attorney for the government will:

(A) not bring, or will move to dismiss, other charges;

(B) recommend, or agree not to oppose the defendant's request, that a particular sentence or sentencing range is appropriate or that a particular provision of the Sentencing Guidelines, or policy statement, or sentencing factor does or does not apply (such a recommendation or request does not bind the court); or

(C) agree that a specific sentence or sentencing range is the appropriate disposition of the case, or that a particular provision of the Sentencing Guidelines, or policy statement, or sentencing factor does or does not apply (such a recommendation or request binds the court once the court accepts the plea agreement).

(2)   Disclosing a Plea Agreement.

The parties must disclose the plea agreement in open court when the plea is offered, unless the court for good cause allows the parties to disclose the plea agreement in camera.

(3)   Judicial Consideration of a Plea Agreement.

(A) To the extent the plea agreement is of the type specified in Rule 11(c)(1)(A) or (C), the court may accept the agreement, reject it, or defer a decision until the court has reviewed the presentence report.

(B) To the extent the plea agreement is of the type specified in Rule 11(c)(1)(B), the court must advise the defendant that the defendant has no right to withdraw the plea if the court does not follow the recommendation or request.

(4)   Accepting a Plea Agreement.

If the court accepts the plea agreement, it must inform the defendant that to the extent the plea agreement is of the type specified in Rule 11(c)(1)(A) or (C), the agreed disposition will be included in the judgment.

(5)   Rejecting a Plea Agreement.

If the court rejects a plea agreement containing provisions of the type specified in Rule 11(c)(1)(A) or (C), the court must do the following on the record and in open court (or, for good cause, in camera):

(A) inform the parties that the court rejects the plea agreement;

(B) advise the defendant personally that the court is not required to follow the plea agreement and give the defendant an opportunity to withdraw the plea; and

(C) advise the defendant personally that if the plea is not withdrawn, the court may dispose of the case less favorably toward the defendant than the plea agreement contemplated.

(d) *Withdrawing a Guilty or Nolo Contendere Plea.*

A defendant may withdraw a plea of guilty or nolo contendere:

(1) before the court accepts the plea, for any reason or no reason; or

(2) after the court accepts the plea, but before it imposes sentence if:

(A) the court rejects a plea agreement under Rule 11(c)(5); or

(**B**) the defendant can show a fair and just reason for requesting the withdrawal.

(e) Finality of a Guilty or Nolo Contendere Plea.

After the court imposes sentence, the defendant may not withdraw a plea of guilty or nolo contendere, and the plea may be set aside only on direct appeal or collateral attack.

(f) Admissibility or Inadmissibility of a Plea, Plea Discussions, and Related Statements.

The admissibility or inadmissibility of a plea, a plea discussion, and any related statement is governed by Federal Rule of Evidence 410.

(g) Recording the Proceedings.

The proceedings during which the defendant enters a plea must be recorded by a court reporter or by a suitable recording device. If there is a guilty plea or a nolo contendere plea, the record must include the inquiries and advice to the defendant required under Rule 11(b) and (c).

(h) Harmless Error.

A variance from the requirements of this rule is harmless error if it does not affect substantial rights.

Rule 14.   Relief from Prejudicial Joinder

(a) Relief.

If the joinder of offenses or defendants in an indictment, an information, or a consolidation for trial appears to prejudice a defendant or the government, the court may order separate trials of counts, sever the defendants' trials, or provide any other relief that justice requires.

(b) Defendant's Statements.

Before ruling on a defendant's motion to sever, the court may order an attorney for the government to deliver to the court for in camera inspection any defendant's statement that the government intends to use as evidence.

Rule 16.   Discovery and Inspection[1]

(a)   Government's Disclosure.

(1)   Information Subject to Disclosure.

(A) Defendant's Oral Statement. Upon a defendant's request, the government must disclose to the defendant the substance of any relevant oral statement made by the defendant, before or after arrest, in response to interrogation by a person the defendant knew was a government agent if the government intends to use the statement at trial.

(B) Defendant's Written or Recorded Statement. Upon a defendant's request, the government must disclose to the defendant, and make available for inspection, copying, or photographing, all of the following:

(i) any relevant written or recorded statement by the defendant if:

- the statement is within the government's possession, custody, or control; and
- the attorney for the government knows—or through due diligence could know—that the statement exists;

(ii) the portion of any written record containing the substance of any relevant oral statement made before or after arrest if the defendant made the statement in response to interrogation by a person the defendant knew was a government agent; and

(iii) the defendant's recorded testimony before a grand jury relating to the charged offense.

(C) Organizational Defendant. Upon a defendant's request, if the defendant is an organization, the government must disclose to the defendant any statement described in Rule 16(a)(1)(A) and (B) if the government contends that the person making the statement:

(i) was legally able to bind the defendant regarding the subject of the statement because of that person's position as the defendant's director, officer, employee, or agent; or

(ii) was personally involved in the alleged conduct constituting the offense and was legally able to bind the defendant regarding that conduct because of that person's position as the defendant's director, officer, employee, or agent.

[1] As amended by changes effective December 1, 2022.

(D) **Defendant's Prior Record.** Upon a defendant's request, the government must furnish the defendant with a copy of the defendant's prior criminal record that is within the government's possession, custody, or control if the attorney for the government knows—or through due diligence could know—that the record exists.

(E) **Documents and Objects.** Upon a defendant's request, the government must permit the defendant to inspect and to copy or photograph books, papers, documents, data, photographs, tangible objects, buildings or places, or copies or portions of any of these items, if the item is within the government's possession, custody, or control and:

(i) the item is material to preparing the defense;

(ii) the government intends to use the item in its case-in-chief at trial; or

(iii) the item was obtained from or belongs to the defendant.

(F) **Reports of Examinations and Tests.** Upon a defendant's request, the government must permit a defendant to inspect and to copy or photograph the results or reports of any physical or mental examination and of any scientific test or experiment if:

(i) the item is within the government's possession, custody, or control;

(ii) the attorney for the government knows—or through due diligence could know—that the item exists; and

(iii) the item is material to preparing the defense or the government intends to use the item in its case-in-chief at trial.

(G) **Expert witnesses.**

(i) Duty to Disclose. At the defendant's request, the government must disclose to the defendant, in writing, the information required by (iii) for any testimony that the government intends to use under Rules 702, 703, or 705 of the Federal Rules of Evidence during its case-in-chief at trial, or during its rebuttal to counter testimony that the defendant has timely disclosed under (b)(1)(C). If the government requests discovery under the second bullet point in (b)(1)(C)(i) and the defendant complies, the government must, at the defendant's request, disclose to the defendant, in writing, the information required by (iii) for testimony that the government intends to use under Rules 702, 703, or 705 on the issue of the defendant's mental condition.

(ii) Time to Disclose. The court, by order or local rule, must set a time for the government to make its disclosures. The time must be sufficiently before trial to provide a fair opportunity for the defendant to meet the government's evidence.

(iii) Contents of the Disclosure. The disclosure for each expert witness must contain:

- a complete statement of all opinions that the government will elicit from the witness in its case-in-chief, or during its rebuttal to counter testimony that the defendant has timely disclosed under (b)(1)(C);
- the bases and reasons for them;
- the witness's qualifications, including a list of all publications authored in the previous 10 years; and
- a list of all other cases in which, during the previous 4 years, the witness has testified as an expert at trial or by deposition.

(iv) Information Previously Disclosed. If the government previously provided a report under (F) that contained information required by (iii), that information may be referred to, rather than repeated, in the expert-witness disclosure.

(v) Signing the Disclosure. The witness must approve and sign the disclosure, unless the government:

- states in the disclosure why it could not obtain the witness's signature through reasonable efforts; or
- has previously provided under (F) a report, signed by the witness, that contains all the opinions and the bases and reasons for them required by (iii).

(vi) Supplementing and Correcting a Disclosure. The government must supplement or correct its disclosures in accordance with (c).

(2)　Information Not Subject to Disclosure.

Except as permitted by Rule 16(a)(1)(A)-(D), (F), and (G), this rule does not authorize the discovery or inspection of reports, memoranda, or other internal government documents made by an attorney for the government or other government agent in connection with investigating or prosecuting the case. Nor does this rule authorize the discovery or inspection of statements made by prospective government witnesses except as provided in 18 U.S.C. §3500.

(3)   Grand Jury Transcripts.

This rule does not apply to the discovery or inspection of a grand jury's recorded proceedings, except as provided in Rules 6, 12(h), 16(a)(1), and 26.2.

(b)   Defendant's Disclosure.

(1)   Information Subject to Disclosure.

(A) Documents and Objects. If a defendant requests disclosure under Rule 16(a)(1)(E) and the government complies, then the defendant must permit the government, upon request, to inspect and to copy or photograph books, papers, documents, data, photographs, tangible objects, buildings or places, or copies or portions of any of these items if:

(i) the item is within the defendant's possession, custody, or control; and

(ii) the defendant intends to use the item in the defendant's case-in-chief at trial.

(B) Reports of Examinations and Tests. If a defendant requests disclosure under Rule 16(a)(1)(F) and the government complies, the defendant must permit the government, upon request, to inspect and to copy or photograph the results or reports of any physical or mental examination and of any scientific test or experiment if:

(i) the item is within the defendant's possession, custody, or control; and

(ii) the defendant intends to use the item in the defendant's case-in-chief at trial, or intends to call the witness who prepared the report and the report relates to the witness's testimony.

(C) Expert Witnesses.

(i) Duty to Disclose. At the government's request, the defendant must disclose, in writing, the information required by (iii) for any testimony the defendant intends to use under Federal Rule of Evidence 702, 703, or 705 during the defendant's case-in-chief, if:

- the defendant requests disclosure under (a)(1)(G) and the government complies; or
- the defendant has given notice under Rule 12.2(b) of an intent to present expert testimony on the defendant's mental condition.

(ii) *Time to Disclose.* The court, by order or local rule, must set a time for the defendant to make the defendant's disclosures. The time must be sufficiently before trial to provide a fair opportunity for the government to meet the defendant's evidence.

(iii) *Contents of Disclosure.* The disclosure for each expert witness must contain:

- a complete statement of all opinions that the defendant will elicit from the witness in the defendant's case-in-chief;
- the bases and reasons for them;
- the witness's qualifications, including a list of all publications authored in the previous 10 years; and
- a list of all other cases in which, during the previous 4 years, the witness has testified as an expert at trial or by deposition.

(iv) *Information Previously Disclosed.* If the defendant previously provided a report under (B) that contained information required by (iii), that information may be referred to, rather than repeated, in the expert-witness disclosure.

(v) *Signing the Disclosure.* The witness must approve and sign the disclosure, unless the defendant:

- states in the disclosure why the defendant could not obtain the witness's signature through reasonable efforts; or
- has previously provided under (F) a report, signed by the witness, that contains all the opinions and the bases and reasons for them required by (iii).

(vi) *Supplementing and Correcting a Disclosure.* The defendant must supplement or correct the defendant's disclosures in accordance with (c).

(2) **Information Not Subject to Disclosure.**

Except for scientific or medical reports, Rule 16(b)(1) does not authorize discovery or inspection of:

(A) reports, memoranda, or other documents made by the defendant, or the defendant's attorney or agent, during the case's investigation or defense; or

(B) a statement made to the defendant, or the defendant's attorney or agent, by:

(i) the defendant;

(ii) a government or defense witness; or

(iii) a prospective government or defense witness.

(c) Continuing Duty to Disclose.

A party who discovers additional evidence or material before or during trial must promptly disclose its existence to the other party or the court if:

(1) the evidence or material is subject to discovery or inspection under this rule; and

(2) the other party previously requested, or the court ordered, its production.

(d) Regulating Discovery.

(1) Protective and Modifying Orders.

At any time the court may, for good cause, deny, restrict, or defer discovery or inspection, or grant other appropriate relief. The court may permit a party to show good cause by a written statement that the court will inspect ex parte. If relief is granted, the court must preserve the entire text of the party's statement under seal.

(2) Failure to Comply.

If a party fails to comply with this rule, the court may:

(A) order that party to permit the discovery or inspection; specify its time, place, and manner; and prescribe other just terms and conditions;

(B) grant a continuance;

(C) prohibit that party from introducing the undisclosed evidence; or

(D) enter any other order that is just under the circumstances.

Rule 23.   Jury or Nonjury Trial

(a) Jury Trial.

If the defendant is entitled to a jury trial, the trial must be by jury unless:

(1) the defendant waives a jury trial in writing;

(2) the government consents; and

(3) the court approves.

(b) Jury Size.

(1)   In General.

A jury consists of 12 persons unless this rule provides otherwise.

(2)   Stipulation for a Smaller Jury.

At any time before the verdict, the parties may, with the court's approval, stipulate in writing that:

(A) the jury may consist of fewer than 12 persons; or

(B) a jury of fewer than 12 persons may return a verdict if the court finds it necessary to excuse a juror for good cause after the trial begins.

(3)   Court Order for a Jury of 11.

After the jury has retired to deliberate, the court may permit a jury of 11 persons to return a verdict, even without a stipulation by the parties, if the court finds good cause to excuse a juror.

(c) Nonjury Trial.

In a case tried without a jury, the court must find the defendant guilty or not guilty. If a party requests before the finding of guilty or not guilty, the court must state its specific findings of fact in open court or in a written decision or opinion.

Rule 26.2.   Producing a Witness's Statement

(a) Motion to Produce.

After a witness other than the defendant has testified on direct examination, the court, on motion of a party who did not call the witness, must order an attorney for the government or the defendant and the defendant's attorney to produce, for the examination and use of the moving party, any statement of the witness that is in their possession and that relates to the subject matter of the witness's testimony.

Rule 41.   Search and Seizure

(a)   Scope and Definitions.

(1)   Scope.

This rule does not modify any statute regulating search or seizure, or the issuance and execution of a search warrant in special circumstances.

(2)   Definitions.

The following definitions apply under this rule:

(**A**) "Property" includes documents, books, papers, any other tangible objects, and information.

(**B**) "Daytime" means the hours between 6:00 a.m. and 10:00 p.m. according to local time.

(**C**) "Federal law enforcement officer" means a government agent (other than an attorney for the government) who is engaged in enforcing the criminal laws and is within any category of officers authorized by the Attorney General to request a search warrant.

(**D**) "Domestic terrorism" and "international terrorism" have the meanings set out in 18 U.S.C. §2331.

(**E**) "Tracking device" has the meaning set out in 18 U.S.C. §3117(b).

(b)   Venue for a Warrant Application

At the request of a federal law enforcement officer or an attorney for the government:

(1) a magistrate judge with authority in the district—or if none is reasonably available, a judge of a state court of record in the district—has authority to

issue a warrant to search for and seize a person or property located within the district;

(2) a magistrate judge with authority in the district has authority to issue a warrant for a person or property outside the district if the person or property is located within the district when the warrant is issued but might move or be moved outside the district before the warrant is executed;

(3) a magistrate judge—in an investigation of domestic terrorism or international terrorism—with authority in any district in which activities related to the terrorism may have occurred has authority to issue a warrant for a person or property within or outside that district; and

(4) a magistrate judge with authority in the district has authority to issue a warrant to install within the district a tracking device; the warrant may authorize use of the device to track the movement of a person or property located within the district, outside the district, or both; and

(5) a magistrate judge having authority in any district where activities related to the crime may have occurred, or in the District of Columbia, may issue a warrant for property that is located outside the jurisdiction of any state or district, but within any of the following:

(A)   a United States territory, possession, or commonwealth;
(B)   the premises—no matter who owns them—of a United States diplomatic or consular mission in a foreign state, including any appurtenant building, part of a building, or land used for the mission's purposes; or
(C)   a residence and any appurtenant land owned or leased by the United States and used by United States personnel assigned to a United States diplomatic or consular mission in a foreign state.

(6) a magistrate with authority in any district where activities related to a crime may have occurred has authority to issue a warrant to use remote access to search electronic storage media and to seize or copy electronically stored information located within or outside that district if:

(A)   the district where the media or information is located has been concealed through technological means; or
(B)   in an investigation of a violation of 18 U.S.C. §1030(a)(5), the media are protected computers that have been damaged without authorization and are located in five or more districts.

(c)   Persons or Property Subject to Search or Seizure.

A warrant may be issued for any of the following:

(1) evidence of a crime;

(2) contraband, fruits of crime, or other items illegally possessed;

(3) property designed for use, intended for use, or used in committing a crime; or

(4) a person to be arrested or a person who is unlawfully restrained.

(d)   Obtaining a Warrant.

(1)   In General.

After receiving an affidavit or other information, a magistrate judge — or if authorized by Rule 41(b), a judge of a state court of record — must issue the warrant if there is probable cause to search for and seize a person or property or to install and use a tracking device.

(2)   Requesting a Warrant in the Presence of a Judge.

(A) In General. A magistrate judge may issue a warrant based on information communicated by telephone or other reliable electronic means.

(B) Recording Testimony. Upon learning that an applicant is requesting a warrant under Rule 41(d)(3)(A), a magistrate judge must:

(i) place under oath the applicant and any person on whose testimony the application is based; and

(ii) make a verbatim record of the conversation with a suitable recording device, if available, or by a court reporter, or in writing.

(C) Recording Testimony. Testimony taken in support of a warrant must be recorded by a court reporter or by a suitable recording device, and the judge must file the transcript or recording with the clerk, along with any affidavit.

   (3)   Requesting a Warrant by Telephonic or Other Means.

In accordance with Rule 4.1, a magistrate judge may issue a warrant based on information communicated by telephone or other reliable electronic means.

   (e)   Issuing the Warrant.

   (1)   In General.

The magistrate judge or a judge of a state court of record must issue the warrant to an officer authorized to execute it.

   (2)   Contents of the Warrant.

(A) Warrant to Search for and Seize a Person or Property. Except for a tracking-device warrant, the warrant must identify the person or property to be searched, identify any person or property to be seized, and designate the magistrate judge to whom it must be returned. The warrant must command the officer to:

   (i) execute the warrant within a specified time no longer than 14 days;

   (ii) execute the warrant during the daytime, unless the judge for good cause expressly authorizes execution at another time; and

   (iii) return the warrant to the magistrate judge designated in the warrant.

(B) Warrant Seeking Electronically Stored Information. A warrant under Rule 41(e)(2)(A) may authorize the seizure of electronic storage media or the seizure or copying of electronically stored information. Unless otherwise specified, the warrant authorizes a later review of the media or information consistent with the warrant. The time for executing the warrant in Rule 4(e)(2)(A) and (f)(1)(A) refers to the seizure or on-site copying of the media or information, and not to any later off-site copying or review.

(C) Warrant for a Tracking Device. A tracking-device warrant must identify the person or property to be tracked, designate the magistrate judge to whom it must be returned, and specify a reasonable length of time that the device may be used. The time must not exceed 45 days from the date the warrant was issued. The court may, for good cause, grant one or more extensions for a reasonable period not to exceed 45 days each. The warrant must command the officer to:

(i) complete any installation authorized by the warrant within a specified time no longer than 10 calendar days;

(ii) perform any installation authorized by the warrant during the daytime, unless the judge for good cause expressly authorizes installation at another time; and

(iii) return the warrant to the judge designated in the warrant.

(f)   Executing and Returning the Warrant.

(1)   Warrant to Search for and Seize a Person or Property.

(A) **Noting the Time.** The officer executing the warrant must enter on it the exact date and time it was executed.

(B) **Inventory.** An officer present during the execution of the warrant must prepare and verify an inventory of any property seized. The officer must do so in the presence of another officer and the person from whom, or from whose premises, the property was taken. If either one is not present, the officer must prepare and verify the inventory in the presence of at least one other credible person. In a case involving the seizure of electronic storage media or the seizure or copying of electronically stored information, the inventory may be limited to describing the physical storage media that were seized or copied. The officer may retain a copy of the electronically stored information that was seized or copied.

(C) **Receipt.** The officer executing the warrant must give a copy of the warrant and a receipt for the property taken to the person from whom, or from whose premises, the property was taken or leave a copy of the warrant and receipt at the place where the officer took the property.

(D) **Return.** The officer executing the warrant must promptly return it—together with a copy of the inventory—to the magistrate judge designated on the warrant. The judge must, on request, give a copy of the inventory to the person from whom, or from whose premises, the property was taken and to the applicant for the warrant.

(2)   Warrant for a Tracking Device.

(A) **Noting the Time.** The officer executing a tracking-device warrant must enter on it the exact date and time the device was installed and the period during which it was used.

(B) Return. Within 10 calendar days after the use of the tracking device has ended, the officer executing the warrant must return it to the judge designated in the warrant.

(C) Service. Within 10 calendar days after the use of the tracking device has ended, the officer executing a tracking-device warrant must serve a copy of the warrant on the person who was tracked or whose property was tracked. Service may be accomplished by delivering a copy to the person who, or whose property, was tracked; or by leaving a copy at the person's residence or usual place of abode with an individual of suitable age and discretion who resides at that location and by mailing a copy to the person's last known address. Upon request of the government, the judge may delay notice as provided in Rule 41(f)(3).

(3)   Delayed Notice.

Upon the government's request, a magistrate judge—or if authorized by Rule 41(b), a judge of a state court of record—may delay any notice required by this rule if the delay is authorized by statute.

(g)   *Motion to Return Property.*

A person aggrieved by an unlawful search and seizure of property or by the deprivation of property may move for the property's return. The motion must be filed in the district where the property was seized. The court must receive evidence on any factual issue necessary to decide the motion. If it grants the motion, the court must return the property to the movant, but may impose reasonable conditions to protect access to the property and its use in later proceedings.

(h)   *Motion to Suppress.*

A defendant may move to suppress evidence in the court where the trial will occur, as Rule 12 provides.

(i)   *Forwarding Papers to the Clerk.*

The magistrate judge to whom the warrant is returned must attach to the warrant a copy of the return, of the inventory, and of all other related papers and must deliver them to the clerk in the district where the property was seized.

Excerpted Statutes

18 U.S.C.

§3142.   RELEASE OR DETENTION OF A DEFENDANT PENDING TRIAL

(a) **In general.** — Upon the appearance before a judicial officer of a person charged with an offense, the judicial officer shall issue an order that, pending trial, the person be —

(1) released on personal recognizance or upon execution of an unsecured appearance bond, under subsection (b) of this section;

(2) released on a condition or combination of conditions under subsection (c) of this section;

(3) temporarily detained to permit revocation of conditional release, deportation, or exclusion under subsection (d) of this section; or

(4) detained under subsection (e) of this section.

(b) **Release on personal recognizance or unsecured appearance bond.** — The judicial officer shall order the pretrial release of the person on personal recognizance, or upon execution of an unsecured appearance bond in an amount specified by the court, subject to the condition that the person not commit a Federal, State, or local crime during the period of release and subject to the condition that the person cooperate in the collection of a DNA sample from the person if the collection of such a sample is authorized pursuant to section 3 of the DNA Analysis Backlog Elimination Act of 2000 (42 U.S.C. §14135a), unless the judicial officer determines that such release will not reasonably assure the appearance of the person as required or will endanger the safety of any other person or the community.

(c) **Release on conditions.** — (1) If the judicial officer determines that the release described in subsection (b) of this section will not reasonably assure the appearance of the person as required or will endanger the safety of any other person or the community, such judicial officer shall order the pretrial release of the person —

(A) subject to the condition that the person not commit a Federal, State, or local crime during the period of release and subject to the condition that the person cooperate in the collection of a DNA sample from the person if the collection of such a sample is authorized pursuant to section 3 of the DNA Analysis Backlog Elimination Act of 2000 (42 U.S.C. §14135a); and

(B) subject to the least restrictive further condition, or combination of conditions, that such judicial officer determines will reasonably assure the appearance of the person as required and the safety of any other person and the community, which may include the condition that the person —

(i) remain in the custody of a designated person, who agrees to assume supervision and to report any violation of a release condition to the court, if the designated person is able reasonably to assure the judicial officer that the person will appear as required and will not pose a danger to the safety of any other person or the community;

(ii) maintain employment, or, if unemployed, actively seek employment;

(iii) maintain or commence an educational program;

(iv) abide by specified restrictions on personal associations, place of abode, or travel;

(v) avoid all contact with an alleged victim of the crime and with a potential witness who may testify concerning the offense;

(vi) report on a regular basis to a designated law enforcement agency, pretrial services agency, or other agency;

(vii) comply with a specified curfew;

(viii) refrain from possessing a firearm, destructive device, or other dangerous weapon;

(ix) refrain from excessive use of alcohol, or any use of a narcotic drug or other controlled substance, as defined in section 102 of the Controlled Substances Act (21 U.S.C. §802), without a prescription by a licensed medical practitioner;

(x) undergo available medical, psychological, or psychiatric treatment, including treatment for drug or alcohol dependency, and remain in a specified institution if required for that purpose;

(xi) execute an agreement to forfeit upon failing to appear as required, property of a sufficient unencumbered value, including money, as is reasonably necessary to assure the appearance of the person as required, and shall provide the court with proof of ownership and the value of the property along with information regarding existing encumbrances as the judicial office may require;

(xii) execute a bail bond with solvent sureties; who will execute an agreement to forfeit in such amount as is reasonably necessary to assure appearance of the person as required and shall provide the court with information regarding the value of the assets and liabilities of the surety if other than an approved surety and the nature and extent of encumbrances against the surety's property; such surety shall have a net worth which shall have sufficient unencumbered value to pay the amount of the bail bond;

(xiii) return to custody for specified hours following release for employment, schooling, or other limited purposes; and

(xiv) satisfy any other condition that is reasonably necessary to assure the appearance of the person as required and to assure the safety of any other person and the community.

In any case that involves a minor victim under section 1201, 1591, 2241, 2242, 2244(a)(1), 2245, 2251, 2251A, 2252(a)(1), 2252(a)(2), 2252(a)(3), 2252A(a)(1), 2252A(a)(2), 2252A(a)(3), 2252A(a)(4), 2260,

2421, 2422, 2423, or 2425 of this title, or a failure to register offense under section 2250 of this title, any release order shall contain, at a minimum, a condition of electronic monitoring and each of the conditions specified at subparagraphs (iv), (v), (vi), (vii), and (viii).

(2) The judicial officer may not impose a financial condition that results in the pretrial detention of the person.

(3) The judicial officer may at any time amend the order to impose additional or different conditions of release.

(d) Temporary detention to permit revocation of conditional release, deportation, or exclusion.—If the judicial officer determines that—

(1) such person—

(A) is, and was at the time the offense was committed, on—

(i) release pending trial for a felony under Federal, State, or local law;

(ii) release pending imposition or execution of sentence, appeal of sentence or conviction, or completion of sentence, for any offense under Federal, State, or local law; or

(iii) probation or parole for any offense under Federal, State, or local law; or

(B) is not a citizen of the United States or lawfully admitted for permanent residence, as defined in section 101(a)(20) of the Immigration and Nationality Act (8 U.S.C. §1101(a)(20)); and

(2) such person may flee or pose a danger to any other person or the community; such judicial officer shall order the detention of such person, for a period of not more than ten days, excluding Saturdays, Sundays, and holidays, and direct the attorney for the Government to notify the appropriate court, probation or parole official, or State or local law enforcement official, or the appropriate official of the Immigration and Naturalization Service. If the official fails or declines to take such person into custody during that period, such person shall be treated in accordance with the other provisions of this section, notwithstanding the applicability of other provisions of law governing release pending trial or deportation or exclusion proceedings. If temporary detention is sought under paragraph (1) (B) of this subsection, such person has the burden of proving to the court such person's United States citizenship or lawful admission for permanent residence.

(e) Detention.—(1) If, after a hearing pursuant to the provisions of subsection (f) of this section, the judicial officer finds that no condition or combination of conditions will reasonably assure the appearance of the person as required and the safety of any other person and the community, such judicial officer shall order the detention of the person before trial.

(2) In a case described in subsection (f)(1) of this section, a rebuttable presumption arises that no condition or combination of conditions will

reasonably assure the safety of any other person and the community if such judicial officer finds that—

(A) the person has been convicted of a Federal offense that is described in subsection (f)(1) of this section, or of a State or local offense that would have been an offense described in subsection (f)(1) of this section if a circumstance giving rise to Federal jurisdiction had existed;

(B) the offense described in subparagraph (A) was committed while the person was on release pending trial for a Federal, State, or local offense; and

(C) a period of not more than five years has elapsed since the date of conviction, or the release of the person from imprisonment, for the offense described in subparagraph (A), whichever is later.

(3) Subject to rebuttal by the person, it shall be presumed that no condition or combination of conditions will reasonably assure the appearance of the person as required and the safety of the community if the judicial officer finds that there is probable cause to believe that the person committed—

(A) an offense for which a maximum term of imprisonment of ten years or more is prescribed in the Controlled Substances Act (21 U.S.C. §801 et seq.), the Controlled Substances Import and Export Act (21 U.S.C. §951 et seq.), or chapter 705 of title 46;

(B) an offense under section 924(c), 956(a), or 2332b of this title;

(C) an offense listed in section 2332b(g)(5)(B) of title 18, United States Code, for which a maximum term of imprisonment of 10 years or more is prescribed;

(D) an offense under chapter 77 of this title for which a maximum term of imprisonment of 20 years or more is prescribed; or

(E) an offense involving a minor victim under section 1201, 1591, 2241, 2242, 2244(a)(1), 2245, 2251, 2251A, 2252(a)(1), 2252(a)(2), 2252(a)(3), 2252A(a)(1), 2252A(a)(2), 2252A(a)(3), 2252A(a)(4), 2260, 2421, 2422, 2423, or 2425 of this title.

(f) **Detention hearing.**—The judicial officer shall hold a hearing to determine whether any condition or combination of conditions set forth in subsection (c) of this section will reasonably assure the appearance of such person as required and the safety of any other person and the community—

(1) upon motion of the attorney for the Government, in a case that involves—

(A) a crime of violence, a violation of section 1591, or an offense listed in section 2332b(g)(5)(B) for which a maximum term of imprisonment of 10 years or more is prescribed;

(B) an offense for which the maximum sentence is life imprisonment or death;

(C) an offense for which a maximum term of imprisonment of ten years or more is prescribed in the Controlled Substances Act (21 U.S.C.

§801 et seq.), the Controlled Substances Import and Export Act (21 U.S.C. §951 et seq.), or chapter 705 of title 46;

(**D**) any felony if such person has been convicted of two or more offenses described in subparagraphs (A) through (C) of this paragraph, or two or more State or local offenses that would have been offenses described in subparagraphs (A) through (C) of this paragraph if a circumstance giving rise to Federal jurisdiction had existed, or a combination of such offenses; or

(**E**) any felony that is not otherwise a crime of violence that involves a minor victim or that involves the possession or use of a firearm or destructive device (as those terms are defined in section 921), or any other dangerous weapon, or involves a failure to register under section 2250 of title 18, United States Code; or

(2) Upon motion of the attorney for the Government or upon the judicial officer's own motion, in a case that involves—

(**A**) a serious risk that such person will flee; or

(**B**) a serious risk that such person will obstruct or attempt to obstruct justice, or threaten, injure, or intimidate, or attempt to threaten, injure, or intimidate, a prospective witness or juror.

The hearing shall be held immediately upon the person's first appearance before the judicial officer unless that person, or the attorney for the Government, seeks a continuance. Except for good cause, a continuance on motion of such person may not exceed five days (not including any intermediate Saturday, Sunday, or legal holiday), and a continuance on motion of the attorney for the Government may not exceed three days (not including any intermediate Saturday, Sunday, or legal holiday). During a continuance, such person shall be detained, and the judicial officer, on motion of the attorney for the Government or sua sponte, may order that, while in custody, a person who appears to be a narcotics addict receive a medical examination to determine whether such person is an addict. At the hearing, such person has the right to be represented by counsel, and, if financially unable to obtain adequate representation, to have counsel appointed. The person shall be afforded an opportunity to testify, to present witnesses, to cross-examine witnesses who appear at the hearing, and to present information by proffer or otherwise. The rules concerning admissibility of evidence in criminal trials do not apply to the presentation and consideration of information at the hearing. The facts the judicial officer uses to support a finding pursuant to subsection (e) that no condition or combination of conditions will reasonably assure the safety of any other person and the community shall be supported by clear and convincing evidence. The person may be detained pending completion of the hearing. The hearing may be reopened, before or after a determination by the judicial officer, at any time before trial if the judicial officer finds that information exists that was not known to the movant at the time of the hearing and that has a material bearing on the issue whether there are conditions of release that will reasonably assure the appearance of such person as required and the safety of any other person and the community.

(g) **Factors to be considered.**—The judicial officer shall, in determining whether there are conditions of release that will reasonably assure the appearance of the person as required and the safety of any other person and the community, take into account the available information concerning—

(1) the nature and circumstances of the offense charged, including whether the offense is a crime of violence, a violation of section 1591, a Federal crime of terrorism, or involves a minor victim or a controlled substance, firearm, explosive, or destructive device;

(2) the weight of the evidence against the person;

(3) the history and characteristics of the person, including—

(A) the person's character, physical and mental condition, family ties, employment, financial resources, length of residence in the community, community ties, past conduct, history relating to drug or alcohol abuse, criminal history, and record concerning appearance at court proceedings; and

(B) whether, at the time of the current offense or arrest, the person was on probation, on parole, or on other release pending trial, sentencing, appeal, or completion of sentence for an offense under Federal, State, or local law; and

(4) the nature and seriousness of the danger to any person or the community that would be posed by the person's release. In considering the conditions of release described in subsection (c)(1)(B)(xi) or (c)(1)(B)(xii) of this section, the judicial officer may upon his own motion, or shall upon the motion of the Government, conduct an inquiry into the source of the property to be designated for potential forfeiture or offered as collateral to secure a bond, and shall decline to accept the designation, or the use as collateral, of property that, because of its source, will not reasonably assure the appearance of the person as required.

(h) **Contents of release order.**—In a release order issued under subsection (b) or (c) of this section, the judicial officer shall—

(1) include a written statement that sets forth all the conditions to which the release is subject, in a manner sufficiently clear and specific to serve as a guide for the person's conduct; and

(2) advise the person of—

(A) the penalties for violating a condition of release, including the penalties for committing an offense while on pretrial release;

(B) the consequences of violating a condition of release, including the immediate issuance of a warrant for the person's arrest; and

(C) sections 1503 of this title (relating to intimidation of witnesses, jurors, and officers of the court), 1510 (relating to obstruction of criminal investigations), 1512 (tampering with a witness, victim, or an informant), and 1513 (retaliating against a witness, victim, or an informant).

(i) Contents of detention order.—In a detention order issued under subsection (e) of this section, the judicial officer shall—

(1) include written findings of fact and a written statement of the reasons for the detention;

(2) direct that the person be committed to the custody of the Attorney General for confinement in a corrections facility separate, to the extent practicable, from persons awaiting or serving sentences or being held in custody pending appeal;

(3) direct that the person be afforded reasonable opportunity for private consultation with counsel; and

(4) direct that, on order of a court of the United States or on request of an attorney for the Government, the person in charge of the corrections facility in which the person is confined deliver the person to a United States marshal for the purpose of an appearance in connection with a court proceeding.

The judicial officer may, by subsequent order, permit the temporary release of the person, in the custody of a United States marshal or another appropriate person, to the extent that the judicial officer determines such release to be necessary for preparation of the person's defense or for another compelling reason.

(j) Presumption of innocence.—Nothing in this section shall be construed as modifying or limiting the presumption of innocence.

§3144.   Release or Detention of a Material Witness

If it appears from an affidavit filed by a party that the testimony of a person is material in a criminal proceeding, and if it is shown that it may become impracticable to secure the presence of the person by subpoena, a judicial officer may order the arrest of the person and treat the person in accordance with the provisions of section 3142 of this title. No material witness may be detained because of inability to comply with any condition of release if the testimony of such witness can adequately be secured by deposition, and if further detention is not necessary to prevent a failure of justice. Release of a material witness may be delayed for a reasonable period of time until the deposition of the witness can be taken pursuant to the Federal Rules of Criminal Procedure.

§3161.   Time Limits and Exclusions

(a) In any case involving a defendant charged with an offense, the appropriate judicial officer, at the earliest practicable time, shall, after consultation with the counsel for the defendant and the attorney for the Government, set the case for trial on a day certain, or list it for trial on a weekly or other short-term trial calendar at a place within the judicial district, so as to assure a speedy trial.

(b) Any information or indictment charging an individual with the commission of an offense shall be filed within thirty days from the date on which such individual was arrested or served with a summons in connection with such charges. If an individual has been charged with a felony in a district in which no grand jury has been in session during such thirty-day period, the period of time for filing of the indictment shall be extended an additional thirty days.

(c)(1) In any case in which a plea of not guilty is entered, the trial of a defendant charged in an information or indictment with the commission of an offense shall commence within seventy days from the filing date (and making public) of the information or indictment, or from the date the defendant has appeared before a judicial officer of the court in which such charge is pending, whichever date last occurs. If a defendant consents in writing to be tried before a magistrate judge on a complaint, the trial shall commence within seventy days from the date of such consent.

(2) Unless the defendant consents in writing to the contrary, the trial shall not commence less than thirty days from the date on which the defendant first appears through counsel or expressly waives counsel and elects to proceed pro se.

(d)(1) If any indictment or information is dismissed upon motion of the defendant, or any charge contained in a complaint filed against an individual is dismissed or otherwise dropped, and thereafter a complaint is filed against such defendant or individual charging him with the same offense or an offense based on the same conduct or arising from the same criminal episode, or an information or indictment is filed charging such defendant with the same offense or an offense based on the same conduct or arising from the same criminal episode, the provisions of subsections (b) and (c) of this section shall be applicable with respect to such subsequent complaint, indictment, or information, as the case may be.

(2) If the defendant is to be tried upon an indictment or information dismissed by a trial court and reinstated following an appeal, the trial shall commence within seventy days from the date the action occasioning the trial becomes final, except that the court retrying the case may extend the period for trial not to exceed one hundred and eighty days from the date the action occasioning the trial becomes final if the unavailability of witnesses or other factors resulting from the passage of time shall make trial within seventy days impractical. The periods of delay enumerated in section 3161(h) are excluded in computing the time limitations specified in this section. The sanctions of section 3162 apply to this subsection.

(e) If the defendant is to be tried again following a declaration by the trial judge of a mistrial or following an order of such judge for a new trial, the trial shall commence within seventy days from the date the action occasioning the retrial becomes final. If the defendant is to be tried again following an appeal or a collateral attack, the trial shall commence within seventy days from the date the action occasioning the retrial becomes final, except that the court retrying the case may extend the period for retrial not to exceed one hundred and eighty days from the date the action occasioning the retrial becomes final if unavailability of witnesses or other factors resulting from passage of time shall make trial within seventy days impractical. The periods of delay enumerated in section 3161(h) are excluded in computing the time limitations specified in this section. The sanctions of section 3162 apply to this subsection.

(f) Notwithstanding the provisions of subsection (b) of this section, for the first twelve-calendar-month period following the effective date of this section as set forth in section 3163(a) of this chapter the time limit imposed with respect to the period between arrest and indictment by subsection (b) of this section shall be sixty days, for the second such twelve-month period such time limit shall be forty-five days and for the third such period such time limit shall be thirty-five days.

(g) Notwithstanding the provisions of subsection (c) of this section, for the first twelve-calendar-month period following the effective date of this section as set forth in section 3163(b) of this chapter, the time limit with respect to the period between arraignment and trial imposed by subsection (c) of this section shall be one hundred and eighty days, for the second such twelve-month period such time limit shall be one hundred and twenty days, and for the third such period such time limit with respect to the period between arraignment and trial shall be eighty days.

(h) The following periods of delay shall be excluded in computing the time within which an information or an indictment must be filed, or in computing the time within which the trial of any such offense must commence:

(1) Any period of delay resulting from other proceedings concerning the defendant, including but not limited to—

(A) delay resulting from any proceeding, including any examinations, to determine the mental competency or physical capacity of the defendant;

(B) delay resulting from trial with respect to other charges against the defendant;

(C) delay resulting from any interlocutory appeal;

(D) delay resulting from any pretrial motion, from the filing of the motion through the conclusion of the hearing on, or other prompt disposition of, such motion;

(E) delay resulting from any proceeding relating to the transfer of a case or the removal of any defendant from another district under the Federal Rules of Criminal Procedure;

(F) delay resulting from transportation of any defendant from another district, or to and from places of examination or hospitalization, except that any time consumed in excess of ten days from the date an order of removal or an order directing such transportation, and the defendant's arrival at the destination shall be presumed to be unreasonable;

(G) delay resulting from consideration by the court of a proposed plea agreement to be entered into by the defendant and the attorney for the Government; and

(H) delay reasonably attributable to any period, not to exceed thirty days, during which any proceeding concerning the defendant is actually under advisement by the court.

(2) Any period of delay during which prosecution is deferred by the attorney for the Government pursuant to written agreement with the defendant, with the approval of the court, for the purpose of allowing the defendant to demonstrate his good conduct.

(3)(A) Any period of delay resulting from the absence or unavailability of the defendant or an essential witness.

(B) For purposes of subparagraph (A) of this paragraph, a defendant or an essential witness shall be considered absent when his whereabouts are unknown and, in addition, he is attempting to avoid apprehension or prosecution or his whereabouts cannot be determined by due diligence. For purposes of such subparagraph, a defendant or an essential witness shall be considered unavailable whenever his whereabouts are known but his presence for trial cannot be obtained by due diligence or he resists appearing at or being returned for trial.

(4) Any period of delay resulting from the fact that the defendant is mentally incompetent or physically unable to stand trial.

(5) If the information or indictment is dismissed upon motion of the attorney for the Government and thereafter a charge is filed against the defendant for the same offense, or any offense required to be joined with that offense, any period of delay from the date the charge was dismissed to the date the time limitation would commence to run as to the subsequent charge had there been no previous charge.

(6) A reasonable period of delay when the defendant is joined for trial with a codefendant as to whom the time for trial has not run and no motion for severance has been granted.

(7)(A) Any period of delay resulting from a continuance granted by any judge on his own motion or at the request of the defendant or his counsel or at the request of the attorney for the Government, if the judge granted such continuance on the basis of his findings that the ends of justice served by taking such action outweigh the best interest of the public and the defendant in a speedy trial. No such period of delay resulting from a continuance granted by the court in accordance with this paragraph shall be excludable under this subsection unless the court sets forth, in the record of the case, either orally or in writing, its reasons for finding that the ends of justice served by the granting of such continuance outweigh the best interests of the public and the defendant in a speedy trial.

(B) The factors, among others, which a judge shall consider in determining whether to grant a continuance under subparagraph (A) of this paragraph in any case are as follows:

(i) Whether the failure to grant such a continuance in the proceeding would be likely to make a continuation of such proceeding impossible, or result in a miscarriage of justice.

(ii) Whether the case is so unusual or so complex, due to the number of defendants, the nature of the prosecution, or the existence of novel questions of fact or law, that it is unreasonable to expect adequate preparation for pretrial proceedings or for the trial itself within the time limits established by this section.

(iii) Whether, in a case in which arrest precedes indictment, delay in the filing of the indictment is caused because the arrest occurs at a time such that it is unreasonable to expect return and filing of the indictment within the period specified in section 3161(b), or because the facts upon which the grand jury must base its determination are unusual or complex.

(iv) Whether the failure to grant such a continuance in a case which, taken as a whole, is not so unusual or so complex as to fall within clause (ii), would deny the defendant reasonable time to obtain counsel, would unreasonably deny the defendant or the Government continuity of counsel, or would deny counsel for the defendant or the attorney for the Government the reasonable time necessary for effective preparation, taking into account the exercise of due diligence.

(C) No continuance under subparagraph (A) of this paragraph shall be granted because of general congestion of the court's calendar, or lack of diligent preparation or failure to obtain available witnesses on the part of the attorney for the Government.

(8) Any period of delay, not to exceed one year, ordered by a district court upon an application of a party and a finding by a preponderance of the evidence that an official request, as defined in section 3292 of this title, has been made for evidence of any such offense and that it reasonably appears, or reasonably appeared at the time the request was made, that such evidence is, or was, in such foreign country.

(i) If trial did not commence within the time limitation specified in section 3161 because the defendant had entered a plea of guilty or nolo contendere subsequently withdrawn to any or all charges in an indictment or information, the defendant shall be deemed indicted with respect to all charges therein contained within the meaning of section 3161, on the day the order permitting withdrawal of the plea becomes final.

(j)(1) If the attorney for the Government knows that a person charged with an offense is serving a term of imprisonment in any penal institution, he shall promptly—

    (A) undertake to obtain the presence of the prisoner for trial; or

    (B) cause a detainer to be filed with the person having custody of the prisoner and request him to so advise the prisoner and to advise the prisoner of his right to demand trial.

(2) If the person having custody of such prisoner receives a detainer, he shall promptly advise the prisoner of the charge and of the prisoner's right to demand trial. If at any time thereafter the prisoner informs the person having custody that he does demand trial, such person shall cause notice to that effect to be sent promptly to the attorney for the Government who caused the detainer to be filed.

(3) Upon receipt of such notice, the attorney for the Government shall promptly seek to obtain the presence of the prisoner for trial.

(4) When the person having custody of the prisoner receives from the attorney for the Government a properly supported request for temporary custody of such prisoner for trial, the prisoner shall be made available to that attorney for the Government (subject, in cases of interjurisdictional transfer, to any right of the prisoner to contest the legality of his delivery).

(k)(1) If the defendant is absent (as defined by subsection (h)(3)) on the day set for trial, and the defendant's subsequent appearance before the court on a bench warrant or other process or surrender to the court occurs more than 21 days after the day set for trial, the defendant shall be deemed to have first appeared before a judicial officer of the court in which the information or indictment is pending within the meaning of subsection (c) on the date of the defendant's subsequent appearance before the court.

(2) If the defendant is absent (as defined by subsection (h)(3)) on the day set for trial, and the defendant's subsequent appearance before the court on a bench warrant or other process or surrender to the court occurs not more than 21 days after the day set for trial, the time limit required by subsection (c), as extended by subsection (h), shall be further extended by 21 days.

28 U.S.C.

§2241. POWER TO GRANT WRIT

(a) Writs of habeas corpus may be granted by the Supreme Court, any justice thereof, the district courts and any circuit judge within their respective jurisdictions. The order of a circuit judge shall be entered in the records of the district court of the district wherein the restraint complained of is had.

(b) The Supreme Court, any justice thereof and any circuit judge may decline to entertain an application for a writ of habeas corpus and may transfer the application for hearing and determination to the district court having jurisdiction to entertain it.

(c) The writ of habeas corpus shall not extend to a prisoner unless

(1) He is in custody under or by color of the authority of the United States or is committed for trial before some court there of; or

(2) He is in custody for an act done or omitted in pursuance of an Act of Congress, or an order, process, judgment or decree of a court or judge of the United States; or

(3) He is in custody in violation of the constitution or laws or treaties of the United States; or

(4) He, being a citizen of a foreign state and domiciled therein is in custody for an act done or omitted under any alleged right, title, authority, privilege, protection, or exemption claimed under the commission, order or sanction of any foreign state, or under color thereof, the validity and effect of which depend upon the law of nations; or

(5) It is necessary to bring him into court to testify or for trial.

(d) Where an application for a writ of habeas corpus is made by a person in custody under the judgment and sentence of a court of a State which contains two or more Federal judicial districts, the application may be filed in the district court for the district wherein such person is in custody or in the district court for the district within which the State court was held which convicted and sentenced him and each of such district courts shall have concurrent jurisdiction to entertain the application. The district court for the district wherein such an application is filed in the exercise of its discretion and in furtherance of justice may transfer the application to the other district court for hearing and determination.

(e)(1) No court, justice, or judge shall have jurisdiction to hear or consider an application for a writ of habeas corpus filed by or on behalf of an alien detained by the United States who has been determined by the United States to have been properly detained as an enemy combatant or is awaiting such determination.

(2) Except as provided in paragraphs (2) and (3) of section 1005(e) of the Detainee Treatment Act of 2005 (10 U.S.C. §801 note), no court, justice, or judge shall have jurisdiction to hear or consider any other action against the United States or its agents relating to any aspect of the detention, transfer, treatment, trial, or conditions of confinement of an alien who is or was detained by the United States and has been determined by the United States to have been properly detained as an enemy combatant or is awaiting such determination.

§2242. APPLICATION

Application for a writ of habeas corpus shall be in writing signed and verified by the person for whose relief it is intended or by someone acting in his behalf.

It shall allege the facts concerning the applicant's commitment or detention, the name of the person who has custody over him and by virtue of what claim or authority, if known.

It may be amended or supplemented as provided in the rules of procedure applicable to civil actions.

If addressed to the Supreme Court, a justice thereof or a circuit judge it shall state the reasons for not making application to the district court of the district in which the applicant is held.

§2243.   Issuance of Writ; Return; Hearing; Decision

A court, justice or judge entertaining an application for a writ of habeas corpus shall forthwith award the writ or issue an order directing the respondent to show cause why the writ should not be granted, unless it appears from the application that the applicant or person detained is not entitled thereto.

The writ, or order to show cause shall be directed to the person having custody of the person detained. It shall be returned within three days unless for good cause additional time, not exceeding twenty days, is allowed.

The person to whom the writ or order is directed shall make a return certifying the true cause of the detention.

When the writ or order is returned a day shall be set for hearing, not more than five days after the return unless for good cause additional time is allowed.

Unless the application for the writ and the return present only issues of law the person to whom the writ is directed shall be required to produce at the hearing the body of the person detained.

The applicant or the person detained may, under oath, deny any of the facts set forth in the return or allege any other material facts.

The return and all suggestions made against it may be amended, by leave of court, before or after being filed.

The court shall summarily hear and determine the facts, and dispose of the matter as law and justice require.

§2244.   Finality of Determination

(a) No circuit or district judge shall be required to entertain an application for a writ of habeas corpus to inquire into the detention of a person pursuant to a judgment of a court of the United States if it appears that the legality of such detention has been determined by a judge or court of the United States on a prior application for a writ of habeas corpus except as provided in section 2255.

(b)(1) A claim presented in a second or successive habeas corpus application under section 2254 that was presented in a prior application shall be dismissed.

(2) A claim presented in a second or successive habeas corpus application under section 2254 that was not presented in a prior application shall be dismissed unless —

(A) the applicant shows that the claim relies on a new rule of constitutional law, made retroactive to cases on collateral review by the Supreme Court, that was previously unavailable; or

(B)(i) the factual predicate for the claim could not have been discovered previously through the exercise of due diligence; and

(ii) the facts underlying the claim, if proven and viewed in light of the evidence as a whole, would be sufficient to establish by clear and convincing evidence that, but for constitutional error, no reasonable factfinder would have found the applicant guilty of the underlying offense.

(3)(A) Before a second or successive application permitted by this section is filed in the district court, the applicant shall move in the appropriate court of appeals for an order authorizing the district court to consider the application.

(B) A motion in the court of appeals for an order authorizing the district court to consider a second or successive application shall be determined by a three-judge panel of the court of appeals.

(C) The court of appeals may authorize the filing of a second or successive application only if it determines that the application makes a prima facie showing that the application satisfies the requirements of this subsection.

(D) The court of appeals shall grant or deny the authorization to file a second or successive application not later than 30 days after the filing of the motion.

(E) The grant or denial of an authorization by a court of appeals to file a second or successive application shall not be appealable and shall not be the subject of a petition for rehearing or for a writ of certiorari.

(4) A district court shall dismiss any claim presented in a second or successive application that the court of appeals has authorized to be filed unless the applicant shows that the claim satisfies the requirements of this section.

(c) In a habeas corpus proceeding brought in behalf of a person in custody pursuant to the judgment of a State court, a prior judgment of the Supreme Court of the United States on an appeal or review by a writ of certiorari at the instance of the prisoner of the decision of such State court, shall be conclusive as to all issues of fact or law with respect to an asserted denial of a Federal right which constitutes ground for discharge in a habeas corpus proceeding, actually adjudicated by the Supreme Court therein, unless the applicant for the writ of habeas corpus shall plead and the court shall find the existence of a material and controlling fact which did not appear in the record of the proceeding in the Supreme Court and the court shall further find that the applicant for the writ of habeas corpus could not have caused such fact to appear in such record by the exercise of reasonable diligence.

(d)(1) A 1-year period of limitation shall apply to an application for a writ of habeas corpus by a person in custody pursuant to the judgment of a State court. The limitation period shall run from the latest of—

   (A) the date on which the judgment became final by the conclusion of direct review or the expiration of the time for seeking such review;

   (B) the date on which the impediment to filing an application created by State action in violation of the Constitution or laws of the United States is removed, if the applicant was prevented from filing by such State action;

   (C) the date on which the constitutional right asserted was initially recognized by the Supreme Court, if the right has been newly recognized by the Supreme Court and made retroactively applicable to cases on collateral review; or

   (D) the date on which the factual predicate of the claim or claims presented could have been discovered through the exercise of due diligence.

   (2) The time during which a properly filed application for State post-conviction or other collateral review with respect to the pertinent judgment or claim is pending shall not be counted toward any period of limitation under this subsection.

§2245.   Certificate of Trial Judge Admissible in Evidence

On the hearing of an application for a writ of habeas corpus to inquire into the legality of the detention of a person pursuant to a judgment the certificate of the judge who presided at the trial resulting in the judgment, setting forth the facts occurring at the trial, shall be admissible in evidence. Copies of the certificate shall be filed with the court in which the application is pending and in the court in which the trial took place.

§2246.   Evidence; Depositions; Affidavits

On application for a writ of habeas corpus, evidence may be taken orally or by deposition, or, in the discretion of the judge, by affidavit. If affidavits are admitted any party shall have the right to propound written interrogatories to the affiants, or to file answering affidavits.

§2247.   Documentary Evidence

On application for a writ of habeas corpus documentary evidence, transcripts of proceedings upon arraignment, plea and sentence and a transcript of the oral testimony introduced on any previous similar application by or in behalf of the same petitioner, shall be admissible in evidence.

§2248. Return or Answer; Conclusiveness

The allegations of a return to the writ of habeas corpus or of an answer to an order to show cause in a habeas corpus proceeding, if not traversed, shall be accepted as true except to the extent that the judge finds from the evidence that they are not true.

§2249. Certified Copies of Indictment, Plea and Judgment; Duty of Respondent

On application for a writ of habeas corpus to inquire into the detention of any person pursuant to a judgment of a court of the United States, the respondent shall promptly file with the court certified copies of the indictment, plea of petitioner and the judgment, or such of them as may be material to the questions raised, if the petitioner fails to attach them to his petition, and same shall be attached to the return to the writ, or to the answer to the order to show cause.

§2250. Indigent Petitioner Entitled to Documents Without Cost

If on any application for a writ of habeas corpus an order has been made permitting the petitioner to prosecute the application in forma pauperis, the clerk of any court of the United States shall furnish to the petitioner without cost certified copies of such documents or parts of the record on file in his office as may be required by order of the judge before whom the application is pending.

§2251. Stay of State Court Proceedings

A justice or judge of the United States before whom a habeas corpus proceeding is pending, may, before final judgment or after final judgment of discharge, or pending appeal, stay any proceeding against the person detained in any State court or by or under the authority of any State for any matter involved in the habeas corpus proceeding.

After the granting of such a stay, any such proceeding in any State court or by or under the authority of any State shall be void. If no stay is granted, any such proceeding shall be as valid as if no habeas corpus proceedings or appeal were pending.

§2252. Notice

Prior to the hearing of a habeas corpus proceeding in behalf of a person in custody of State officers or by virtue of State laws notice shall be served on the attorney general or other appropriate officer of such State as the justice or judge at the time of issuing the writ shall direct.

§2253.   APPEAL

(a) In a habeas corpus proceeding or a proceeding under section 2255 before a district judge, the final order shall be subject to review, on appeal, by the court of appeals for the circuit in which the proceeding is held.

(b) There shall be no right of appeal from a final order in a proceeding to test the validity of a warrant to remove to another district or place for commitment or trial a person charged with a criminal offense against the United States, or to test the validity of such person's detention pending removal proceedings.

(c)(1) Unless a circuit justice or judge issues a certificate of appealability, an appeal may not be taken to the court of appeals from—

(A) the final order in a habeas corpus proceeding in which the detention complained of arises out of process issued by a State court; or

(B) the final order in a proceeding under section 2255.

(2) A certificate of appealability may issue under paragraph (1) only if the applicant has made a substantial showing of the denial of a constitutional right.

(3) The certificate of appealability under paragraph (1) shall indicate which specific issue or issues satisfy the showing required by paragraph (2).

§2254.   STATE CUSTODY; REMEDIES IN STATE COURTS

(a) The Supreme Court, a Justice thereof, a circuit judge, or a district court shall entertain an application for a writ of habeas corpus in behalf of a person in custody pursuant to the judgment of a State court only on the ground that he is in custody in violation of the Constitution or laws or treaties of the United States.

(b)(1) An application for a writ of habeas corpus on behalf of a person in custody pursuant to the judgment of a State court shall not be granted unless it appears that—

(A) the applicant has exhausted the remedies available in the courts of the State; or

(B)(i) there is an absence of available State corrective process; or

(ii) circumstances exist that render such process ineffective to protect the rights of the applicant.

(2) An application for a writ of habeas corpus may be denied on the merits, notwithstanding the failure of the applicant to exhaust the remedies available in the courts of the State.

(3) A State shall not be deemed to have waived the exhaustion requirement or be estopped from reliance upon the requirement unless the State, through counsel, expressly waives the requirement.

(c) An applicant shall not be deemed to have exhausted the remedies available in the courts of the State, within the meaning of this section, if he has the right under the law of the State to raise, by any available procedure, the question presented.

(d) An application for a writ of habeas corpus on behalf of a person in custody pursuant to the judgment of a State court shall not be granted with respect to any claim that was adjudicated on the merits in State court proceedings unless the adjudication of the claim—

(1) resulted in a decision that was contrary to, or involved an unreasonable application of, clearly established Federal law, as determined by the Supreme Court of the United States; or

(2) resulted in a decision that was based on an unreasonable determination of the facts in light of the evidence presented in the State court proceeding.

(e)(1) In a proceeding instituted by an application for a writ of habeas corpus by a person in custody pursuant to the judgment of a State court, a determination of a factual issue made by a State court shall be presumed to be correct. The applicant shall have the burden of rebutting the presumption of correctness by clear and convincing evidence.

(2) If the applicant has failed to develop the factual basis of a claim in State court proceedings, the court shall not hold an evidentiary hearing on the claim unless the applicant shows that—

(A) the claim relies on—

(i) a new rule of constitutional law, made retroactive to cases on collateral review by the Supreme Court, that was previously unavailable; or

(ii) a factual predicate that could not have been previously discovered through the exercise of due diligence; and

(B) the facts underlying the claim would be sufficient to establish by clear and convincing evidence that but for constitutional error, no reasonable factfinder would have found the applicant guilty of the underlying offense.

(f) If the applicant challenges the sufficiency of the evidence adduced in such State court proceeding to support the State court's determination of a factual issue made therein, the applicant, if able, shall produce that part of the record pertinent to a determination of the sufficiency of the evidence to support such determination. If the applicant, because of indigency or other reason is unable to produce such part of the record, then the State shall produce such part of the record and the Federal court shall direct the State to do so by order directed to an appropriate State official. If the State cannot provide such pertinent part of the record, then the court shall determine under the existing facts and circumstances what weight shall be given to the State court's factual determination.

(g) A copy of the official records of the State court, duly certified by the clerk of such court to be a true and correct copy of a finding, judicial opinion, or other reliable written indicia showing such a factual determination by the State court shall be admissible in the Federal court proceeding.

(h) Except as provided in section 408 of the Controlled Substances Act, in all proceedings brought under this section, and any subsequent proceedings on review, the court may appoint counsel for an applicant who is or becomes financially unable to afford counsel, except as provided by a rule promulgated by the Supreme Court pursuant to statutory authority. Appointment of counsel under this section shall be governed by section 3006A of title 18.

(i) The ineffectiveness or incompetence of counsel during Federal or State collateral post-conviction proceedings shall not be a ground for relief in a proceeding arising under section 2254.

§2255. Federal Custody; Remedies on Motion Attacking Sentence

(a) A prisoner in custody under sentence of a court established by Act of Congress claiming the right to be released upon the ground that the sentence was imposed in violation of the Constitution or laws of the United States, or that the court was without jurisdiction to impose such sentence, or that the sentence was in excess of the maximum authorized by law, or is otherwise subject to collateral attack, may move the court which imposed the sentence to vacate, set aside or correct the sentence.

(b) Unless the motion and the files and records of the case conclusively show that the prisoner is entitled to no relief, the court shall cause notice thereof to be served upon the United States attorney, grant a prompt hearing thereon, determine the issues and make findings of fact and conclusions of law with respect thereto. If the court finds that the judgment was rendered without jurisdiction, or that the sentence imposed was not authorized by law or otherwise open to collateral attack, or that there has been such a denial or infringement of the constitutional rights of the prisoner as to render the judgment vulnerable to collateral attack, the court shall vacate and set the judgment aside and shall discharge the prisoner or resentence him or grant a new trial or correct the sentence as may appear appropriate.

(c) A court may entertain and determine such motion without requiring the production of the prisoner at the hearing.

(d) An appeal may be taken to the court of appeals from the order entered on the motion as from a final judgment on application for a writ of habeas corpus.

(e) An application for a writ of habeas corpus in behalf of a prisoner who is authorized to apply for relief by motion pursuant to this section, shall not be entertained if it appears that the applicant has failed to apply for relief, by motion, to the court which sentenced him, or that such court has denied him relief, unless it also appears that the remedy by motion is inadequate or ineffective to test the legality of his detention.

(f) A 1-year period of limitation shall apply to a motion under this section. The limitation period shall run from the latest of—

(1) the date on which the judgment of conviction becomes final;

(2) the date on which the impediment to making a motion created by governmental action in violation of the Constitution or laws of the United States is removed, if the movant was prevented from making a motion by such governmental action;

(3) the date on which the right asserted was initially recognized by the Supreme Court, if that right has been newly recognized by the Supreme Court and made retroactively applicable to cases on collateral review; or

(4) the date on which the facts supporting the claim or claims presented could have been discovered through the exercise of due diligence.

(g) Except as provided in section 408 of the Controlled Substances Act, in all proceedings brought under this section, and any subsequent proceedings on review, the court may appoint counsel, except as provided by a rule promulgated by the Supreme Court pursuant to statutory authority. Appointment of counsel under this section shall be governed by section 3006A of title 18.

(h) A second or successive motion must be certified as provided in section 2244 by a panel of the appropriate court of appeals to contain—

(1) newly discovered evidence that, if proven and viewed in light of the evidence as a whole, would be sufficient to establish by clear and convincing evidence that no reasonable factfinder would have found the movant guilty of the offense; or

(2) a new rule of constitutional law, made retroactive to cases on collateral review by the Supreme Court, that was previously unavailable.

§2261. Prisoners in State Custody Subject to Capital Sentence; Appointment of Counsel; Requirement of Rule of Court or Statute; Procedures for Appointment

(a) This chapter shall apply to cases arising under section 2254 brought by prisoners in State custody who are subject to a capital sentence. It shall apply only if the provisions of subsections (b) and (c) are satisfied.

(b) **Counsel.**—This chapter is applicable if—

(1) the Attorney General of the United States certifies that a State has established a mechanism for providing counsel in postconviction proceedings as provided in section 2265; and

(2) counsel was appointed pursuant to that mechanism, petitioner validly waived counsel, petitioner retained counsel, or petitioner was found not to be indigent.

(c) Any mechanism for the appointment, compensation, and reimbursement of counsel as provided in subsection (b) must offer counsel to all State prisoners under capital sentence and must provide for the entry of an order by a court of record—

(1) appointing one or more counsels to represent the prisoner upon a finding that the prisoner is indigent and accepted the offer or is unable competently to decide whether to accept or reject the offer;

(2) finding, after a hearing if necessary, that the prisoner rejected the offer of counsel and made the decision with an understanding of its legal consequences; or

(3) denying the appointment of counsel upon a finding that the prisoner is not indigent.

(d) No counsel appointed pursuant to subsections (b) and (c) to represent a State prisoner under capital sentence shall have previously represented the prisoner at trial in the case for which the appointment is made unless the prisoner and counsel expressly request continued representation.

(e) The ineffectiveness or incompetence of counsel during State or Federal post-conviction proceedings in a capital case shall not be a ground for relief in a proceeding arising under section 2254. This limitation shall not preclude the appointment of different counsel, on the court's own motion or at the request of the prisoner, at any phase of State or Federal post-conviction proceedings on the basis of the ineffectiveness or incompetence of counsel in such proceedings.

§2262. MANDATORY STAY OF EXECUTION; DURATION; LIMITS ON STAYS OF EXECUTION; SUCCESSIVE PETITIONS

(a) Upon the entry in the appropriate State court of record of an order under section 2261(c), a warrant or order setting an execution date for a State prisoner shall be stayed upon application to any court that would have jurisdiction over any proceedings filed under section 2254. The application shall recite that the State has invoked the post-conviction review procedures of this chapter and that the scheduled execution is subject to stay.

(b) A stay of execution granted pursuant to subsection (a) shall expire if—

(1) a State prisoner fails to file a habeas corpus application under section 2254 within the time required in section 2263;

(2) before a court of competent jurisdiction, in the presence of counsel, unless the prisoner has competently and knowingly waived such counsel, and after having been advised of the consequences, a State prisoner under capital sentence waives the right to pursue habeas corpus review under section 2254; or

(3) a State prisoner files a habeas corpus petition under section 2254 within the time required by section 2263 and fails to make a substantial showing of the denial of a Federal right or is denied relief in the district court or at any subsequent stage of review.

(c) If one of the conditions in subsection (b) has occurred, no Federal court thereafter shall have the authority to enter a stay of execution in the case, unless the court of appeals approves the filing of a second or successive application under section 2244 (b).

§2263. Filing of Habeas Corpus Application; Time Requirements; Tolling Rules

(a) Any application under this chapter for habeas corpus relief under section 2254 must be filed in the appropriate district court not later than 180 days after final State court affirmance of the conviction and sentence on direct review or the expiration of the time for seeking such review.

(b) The time requirements established by subsection (a) shall be tolled—

(1) from the date that a petition for certiorari is filed in the Supreme Court until the date of final disposition of the petition if a State prisoner files the petition to secure review by the Supreme Court of the affirmance of a capital sentence on direct review by the court of last resort of the State or other final State court decision on direct review;

(2) from the date on which the first petition for post-conviction review or other collateral relief is filed until the final State court disposition of such petition; and

(3) during an additional period not to exceed 30 days, if—

(A) a motion for an extension of time is filed in the Federal district court that would have jurisdiction over the case upon the filing of a habeas corpus application under section 2254; and

(B) a showing of good cause is made for the failure to file the habeas corpus application within the time period established by this section.

§2264. Scope of Federal Review; District Court Adjudications

(a) Whenever a State prisoner under capital sentence files a petition for habeas corpus relief to which this chapter applies, the district court shall only consider a claim or claims that have been raised and decided on the merits in the State courts, unless the failure to raise the claim properly is—

(1) the result of State action in violation of the Constitution or laws of the United States;

(2) the result of the Supreme Court's recognition of a new Federal right that is made retroactively applicable; or

(3) based on a factual predicate that could not have been discovered through the exercise of due diligence in time to present the claim for State or Federal post-conviction review.

(b) Following review subject to subsections (a), (d), and (e) of section 2254, the court shall rule on the claims properly before it.

§2265. CERTIFICATION AND JUDICIAL REVIEW

(a) Certification.—

(1) **In general.**—If requested by an appropriate State official, the Attorney General of the United States shall determine—

(A) whether the State has established a mechanism for the appointment, compensation, and payment of reasonable litigation expenses of competent counsel in State postconviction proceedings brought by indigent prisoners who have been sentenced to death;

(B) the date on which the mechanism described in subparagraph (A) was established; and

(C) whether the State provides standards of competency for the appointment of counsel in proceedings described in subparagraph (A).

(2) **Effective date.**—The date the mechanism described in paragraph (1)(A) was established shall be the effective date of the certification under this subsection.

(3) **Only express requirements.**—There are no requirements for certification or for application of this chapter other than those expressly stated in this chapter.

(b) **Regulations.**—The Attorney General shall promulgate regulations to implement the certification procedure under subsection (a).

(c) **Review of certification.**—

(1) **In general.**—The determination by the Attorney General regarding whether to certify a State under this section is subject to review exclusively as provided under chapter 158 of this title.

(2) **Venue.**—The Court of Appeals for the District of Columbia Circuit shall have exclusive jurisdiction over matters under paragraph (1), subject to review by the Supreme Court under section 2350 of this title.

(3) **Standard of review.**—The determination by the Attorney General regarding whether to certify a State under this section shall be subject to de novo review.

§2266. LIMITATION PERIODS FOR DETERMINING APPLICATIONS AND
        MOTIONS

(a) The adjudication of any application under section 2254 that is subject to this chapter, and the adjudication of any motion under section 2255 by a person under sentence of death, shall be given priority by the district court and by the court of appeals over all noncapital matters.

(b)(1)(A) A district court shall render a final determination and enter a final judgment on any application for a writ of habeas corpus brought under this chapter in a capital case not later than 450 days after the date on which the application is filed, or 60 days after the date on which the case is submitted for decision, whichever is earlier.

(B) A district court shall afford the parties at least 120 days in which to complete all actions, including the preparation of all pleadings and briefs, and if necessary, a hearing, prior to the submission of the case for decision.

(C)(i) A district court may delay for not more than one additional 30-day period beyond the period specified in subparagraph (A), the rendering of a determination of an application for a writ of habeas corpus if the court issues a written order making a finding, and stating the reasons for the finding, that the ends of justice that would be served by allowing the delay outweigh the best interests of the public and the applicant in a speedy disposition of the application.

(ii) The factors, among others, that a court shall consider in determining whether a delay in the disposition of an application is warranted are as follows:

(I) Whether the failure to allow the delay would be likely to result in a miscarriage of justice.

(II) Whether the case is so unusual or so complex, due to the number of defendants, the nature of the prosecution, or the existence of novel questions of fact or law, that it is unreasonable to expect adequate briefing within the time limitations established by subparagraph (A).

(III) Whether the failure to allow a delay in a case that, taken as a whole, is not so unusual or so complex as described in subclause (II), but would otherwise deny the applicant reasonable time to obtain counsel, would unreasonably deny the applicant or the government continuity of counsel, or would deny counsel for the applicant or the government the reasonable time necessary for effective preparation, taking into account the exercise of due diligence.

(iii) No delay in disposition shall be permissible because of general congestion of the court's calendar.

(iv) The court shall transmit a copy of any order issued under clause (i) to the Director of the Administrative Office of the United States Courts for inclusion in the report under paragraph (5).

(2) The time limitations under paragraph (1) shall apply to—

(A) an initial application for a writ of habeas corpus;

(B) any second or successive application for a writ of habeas corpus; and

(C) any redetermination of an application for a writ of habeas corpus following a remand by the court of appeals or the Supreme Court for further proceedings, in which case the limitation period shall run from the date the remand is ordered.

(3)(A) The time limitations under this section shall not be construed to entitle an applicant to a stay of execution, to which the applicant would otherwise not be entitled, for the purpose of litigating any application or appeal.

(B) No amendment to an application for a writ of habeas corpus under this chapter shall be permitted after the filing of the answer to the application, except on the grounds specified in section 2244 (b).

(4)(A) The failure of a court to meet or comply with a time limitation under this section shall not be a ground for granting relief from a judgment of conviction or sentence.

(B) The State may enforce a time limitation under this section by petitioning for a writ of mandamus to the court of appeals. The court of appeals shall act on the petition for a writ of mandamus not later than 30 days after the filing of the petition.

(5)(A) The Administrative Office of the United States Courts shall submit to Congress an annual report on the compliance by the district courts with the time limitations under this section.

(B) The report described in subparagraph (A) shall include copies of the orders submitted by the district courts under paragraph (1)(B)(iv).

(c)(1)(A) A court of appeals shall hear and render a final determination of any appeal of an order granting or denying, in whole or in part, an application brought under this chapter in a capital case not later than 120 days after the date on which the reply brief is filed, or if no reply brief is filed, not later than 120 days after the date on which the answering brief is filed.

(B)(i) A court of appeals shall decide whether to grant a petition for rehearing or other request for rehearing en banc not later than 30 days after the date on which the petition for rehearing is filed unless a responsive pleading is required, in which case the court shall decide whether to grant the petition not later than 30 days after the date on which the responsive pleading is filed.

(ii) If a petition for rehearing or rehearing en banc is granted, the court of appeals shall hear and render a final determination of the appeal not later than 120 days after the date on which the order granting rehearing or rehearing en banc is entered.

(2) The time limitations under paragraph (1) shall apply to—

(A) an initial application for a writ of habeas corpus;

(B) any second or successive application for a writ of habeas corpus; and

(C) any redetermination of an application for a writ of habeas corpus or related appeal following a remand by the court of appeals en banc or the Supreme Court for further proceedings, in which case the limitation period shall run from the date the remand is ordered.

(3) The time limitations under this section shall not be construed to entitle an applicant to a stay of execution, to which the applicant would otherwise not be entitled, for the purpose of litigating any application or appeal.

(4)(A) The failure of a court to meet or comply with a time limitation under this section shall not be a ground for granting relief from a judgment of conviction or sentence.

(B) The State may enforce a time limitation under this section by applying for a writ of mandamus to the Supreme Court.

(5) The Administrative Office of the United States Courts shall submit to Congress an annual report on the compliance by the courts of appeals with the time limitations under this section.